THE
MAN
IN THE
RED
VELVET
DRESS

THE MAN IN THE RED VELVET DRESS

Inside the World of Cross-Dressing

J. J. ALLEN

A BIRCH LANE PRESS BOOK
Published by Carol Publishing Group

A Birch Lane Press Book
Published by Carol Publishing Group
Birch Lane Press is a registered trademark of Carol Communications, Inc.
Editorial Offices: 600 Madison Avenue, New York, N.Y. 10022
Sales and Distribution Offices: 120 Enterprise Avenue, Secaucus, N.J. 07094
In Canada: Canadian Manda Group, One Atlantic Avenue, Suite 105, Toronto,
Ontario M6K 3E7
Queries regarding rights and permissions should be addressed to Carol Publishing
Group, 600 Madison Avenue, New York, N.Y. 10022

Carol Publishing Group books are available at special discounts for bulk purchases,
sales promotion, fund-raising, or educational purposes. Special editions can be
created to specifications. For details, contact: Special Sales Department, Carol
Publishing Group, 120 Enterprise Avenue, Secaucus, N.J. 07094

Manufactured in the United States of America
10 9 8 7 6 5 4 3 2 1

Library of Congress Cataloging-in-Publication Data

Allen, J. J.
    The man in the red velvet dress : inside the world of cross-dressing / J. J. Allen.
        p.   cm.
    "A Birch Lane Press book."
    ISBN 1-55972-338-6 (hardcover)
    1. Transvestism—United States.   2. Transvestites—United States.
I. Title.
HQ77.A29   1996
306.77—dc20   95-50096
                                                                   CIP

It can be very difficult for a woman to be married to a cross-dresser. The same could be said of any person who is married to a writer. My wife happens to be married to both. For her understanding, courage, and love, I dedicate this book to her.

CONTENTS

THE
MAN
IN THE
RED
VELVET
DRESS

1

THE NINE REASONS MEN CROSS-DRESS

It came in the mail on Monday: an engraved invitation to attend a private party that Friday evening at a popular Hollywood nightclub. My friend Angel had also been invited. She dared me to do it. "You paid enough for that dress, you might as well wear it," she insisted.

I replied that I wasn't quite ready to wear the dress in public.

"Look," she reasoned, "in this day and age a man should be able to wear a dress to a chic Hollywood party. And besides, you know you've been dying to wear it since you bought it."

She was right. I decided to go dressed as my alter ego, Justine Sahnjay. While I had been to other events dressed like a woman, this party would certainly be the most challenging.

"Is that a man in the red velvet dress?" a woman not so discreetly asked her friends as I entered the party. People usually see cross-dressers only on talk shows; they seldom get to meet the real thing. I soon found myself surrounded by curious people.

The inevitable question quickly arose. "Why do you enjoy dressing like a woman?" an older lady asked. I spent a few minutes trying to answer her question, but it only led to more questions. She soon realized what I had come to know: Cross-dressing is a fairly sophisticated subject. "Maybe you should write a book about cross-dressing," she suggested in an offhand manner.

I thought I just might. After all, there's only a handful of books on the topic, and most of those are either academic works or true confessions. The academic stuff is not all that interesting, and the true-confession books tend to be tales of transsexual suffering. It was at that party that I decided to tell the story of cross-dressing from the perspective of the man in the red velvet dress.

Where does one begin to talk about cross-dressing? The best place to go is to recent events in the news. For example, after a hidden camera caught him stealing Marla Trump's high heels and lingerie, her former publicist admitted that he had "a sexual relationship" with her shoes. How does a man reach the point where he can have a sexual relationship with a pair of high heels, panties, or other articles of women's clothing? And why would a man risk arrest for stealing heels or lingerie when he could easily buy such things at the mall? Exploring the circuitous route whereby man and shoe meet and fall in love is difficult enough, but what about men who go beyond shoes? What about men who cross-dress fully as women, or who try to become women through hormones and surgery?

Society is undecided about cross-dressers because it doesn't know much about them. As a longtime cross-dresser (CD) and past president of Powder Puff of California (PPOC), a Los Angeles area CD support group, my intention in writing this book is to offer the reader an inside view of the motives, psyche, sexuality, and social world of the male CD.

Written from the perspective I've gained in living a part of life that most people will never experience, the book is personal rather than academic. While I will touch upon the clinical aspects of fetishism and cross-dressing, I leave the bulk of the psychological, cross-cultural, and statistical aspects of my topic to the scholars.

Humor has always been an important element for me in keeping cross-dressing in perspective. For this reason, I'll be including selections from the column I wrote for the PPOC newsletter throughout the book. Entitled "The TV Social Register," the column aimed at satirizing both the cross-dressing community and society.

THE KEY QUESTION

What motivates the CD? CDs are frequently seen on talk shows, and you may have even occasionally spotted one at the mall. They have been featured through the years in hit movies such as *Some Like It Hot, Tootsie, The Crying Game, Mrs. Doubtfire,* and *To Wong Foo, Thanks for Everything, Julie Newmar!* Men who dress like women provoke society's curiosity because the motivation for their behavior is puzzling.

I believe I can safely state that I speak for every CD when I say that I've been trying to figure out why I cross-dress for most of my life. My search has taken me into both Eastern and Western religion, philosophy, intense therapy, and the sexual underground in Los Angeles. Having had a tremendous struggle with cross-dressing, both as an adolescent with my parents, and within the context of romance and marriage, I can testify that it's not easy for a man to come to terms with the fact that he's a CD, let alone understand why he is.

That the CD himself has trouble accepting or understanding his behavior makes it that much more difficult for an outsider to fathom. The January 16, 1995, issue of *The New Yorker* included an article on the subject of cross-dressing by John Berendt, author of the bestselling *Midnight in the Garden of Good and Evil.* Entitled "High Heel Neil," Berendt's article profiled the noted Nashville business tycoon and public CD Neil Cargile.

Berendt attempted to answer the question of why Neil Cargile cross-dresses. Throughout the article, the flamboyant Cargile, famous for wearing outrageous female outfits in public, flaunts his transvestism in front of a perplexed society while managing to frustrate Berendt's powers of investigation. It is one thing for a novelist to define the characters in his book; it is quite another for him to define a wealthy, boisterous, sixty-one-year-old transvestite who will neither behave properly nor explain his misbehavior.

Cargile and his girlfriend, for instance, met Berendt for lunch at the tony Central Park restaurant, Tavern on the Green. Cargile made a grand entrance wearing a blazer and an open-necked shirt, along with a "black-and-white striped micro-miniskirt, pantyhose, and heels." Heads turned, mouths dropped, people murmured. The traffic past the Berendt-Cargile table mounted as fellow diners streamed by—ostensibly on the way to the restroom—to get a better view of Cargile. Berendt's embarrassment was such that he remarked, "At that moment I would have given anything to cover my head with a large napkin."

The only answer that Cargile would offer for his cross-dressing was that "it's fun." Berendt was unable to coax any other insight from High Heel Neil. The reader is left wondering, as was Berendt, why some men cross-dress. Surely there must be a more profound explanation for this behavior than mere fun.

DEFINING CROSS-DRESSING

Before I address a catalogue of motivations, I will define the term *cross-dresser*. A cross-dresser is a person who dresses in the clothing of the opposite sex. Yet there is a continuum in the world of cross-dressing that stretches from the fetishist to the postoperative transsexual. It is therefore important to understand that the term *cross-dresser* describes only a common characteristic seen within a broad range of motivations and behaviors.

Other terms have been offered to describe the CD. The classic term *transvestite* was coined in 1910 by the German sexologist Magnus Hirschfield. The word is a combining of the Latin *trans* meaning "across" and *vestire* meaning "clothing"—hence, a transvestite is one who "dresses across" from his or her normal sex.

Eonism, another word used to describe cross-dressing, is derived from the name of the French diplomat, the Chevalier D'Eon (1728–1810). D'Eon began adult life as a soldier, became a diplomat who often performed diplomatic duties while cross-dressed, and then went on to become an actress.

As D'Eon was well known for his military and political career, his entry into the theater as an actress caused quite a stir. This would not be unlike, say, former NATO commander and secretary of state Alexander Haig becoming an actress. (Well, you do have to admit that Haig might look sort of like Joan Crawford if he donned a wig and pearls.) The early sexologist Havelock Ellis coined the term *eonism* to describe cross-dressing, but Ellis's term never became fashionable to describe the sport.

Female impersonator is a term applied primarily to stage performers who limit their cross-dressing to the stage. *Drag queen* is a generally pejorative term used to describe transvestite prostitutes and those CDs who dress in a highly sexualized and fetishistic fashion.

Many advanced practitioners of cross-dressing, particularly those who dress and live full-time as women, prefer a term that places emphasis on gender rather than sex. *Transgenderist,* a term coined by Virginia Prince, the founder of the modern CD movement, is currently in vogue to describe CDs. Transgenderism, with its emphasis on the distinction between sex and gender, is discussed in chapters 4 and 5.

Others within the transgendered community have offered a different term which they feel speaks more precisely to their situation. *Dysphoric* is the antonym of *euphoric.* Hence, *gender dysphoria* is a coined term used to describe a condition in which a person is persistently unhappy with his born anatomical sex. Gender dysphoria can occur in both heterosexuals and homosexuals, thus indicating that sexual preference is not an overriding factor in the condition.

One could endlessly invent new words in an attempt to capture the essence of the experience. But given that there are so many hues within cross-dressing and related gender issues, no single term would please everyone. I prefer to use the simple and popular term *cross-dresser* because it conveys the most obvious characteristic of the behavior. Likewise, the term *transgender community* is suitable to describe that segment of the population that is concerned with matters relating to gender freedom.

THE RIDDLE OF CROSS-DRESSING

Cross-dressing is a puzzling behavior that encompasses a wide range of psychological, sexual, and cultural complexities. That it engenders such a high level of curiosity, interest, concern, ridicule, and even fear indicates that it is an issue far from being resolved; people just don't know what to make of it. The CD both intrigues and threatens because he breaks one of the fundamental rules of our culture: *Men are not supposed to dress or act like women.*

Talk shows have dealt widely with the topic of cross-dressing, and the programs are generally predictable. You'll see a sober cross-dresser and his wife and two flaming, gay drag queens. By contrasting the seemingly respectable married man, whom you'd never suspect of being a CD, with the drag queens, the talk shows only serve to heighten the ambivalence about cross-dressing: Is the true CD a stable, middle-aged, married white-collar worker or is he a flamboyant, effeminate homosexual who takes female hormones and has breast implants?

Books about cross-dressing are not much better than the talk shows, for they're either serious psychological and sociological works, true confessions, or mere pornography. A comprehensive bibliography of cross-dressing would offer titles ranging from *Panty-Clad Prisoner* and *Destined for Dresses* to *Costumes of the Mind: Transvestism as a Metaphor in Modern Literature* and *Vested Interests: Cross-Dressing and Cultural Anxiety.*

Yet this ambivalence is not unique to cross-dressing, for when it comes to dealing with their sexuality people seem to want either therapy, catharsis, or pornography. Indeed, the question "Am I normal, disturbed, or merely obscene?" is asked by many people when they consider their sexuality. However, the sexual ambivalence surrounding cross-dressing seems more intense because the behavior is unconventional. Due to the lack of readily available and reliable information, people often turn to newspaper columnists for advice when they first suspect a problem with a family member. The following letter could be written to any advice columnist:

Dear Amy:

My husband, I'll call him John, stayed home "sick" from work today. I came home unexpectedly at noon to bring him lunch. I went into the house quietly because I didn't want to wake John up in case he was sleeping. It was quiet in the house so I went upstairs to check on him. Imagine my shock when I opened the bedroom door and found John standing in front of our bedroom mirror masturbating while wearing my black lace panties and bra. He also had on a black garter belt, stockings, and a pair of high heels, all of which he said he had purchased through a mail-order catalogue. He confided to me that he has always liked to wear women's clothing. I'm upset and don't know what to think. Should he get therapy? Is he gay? Please help.

Signed,
Confused With Laundry to Do in Los Angeles

How would you answer John's wife? Is John normal, in need of therapy, or gay? Or are there other possible answers to the riddle of men who wear women's clothing? Nobody really knows why certain men cross-dress. One of the nation's leading authorities on the topic, Dr. Richard F. Docter, said in the preface to his excellent book *Transvestites and Transsexuals: Toward a Theory of Cross-Gender Behavior:*

> I agree with other gender researchers . . . who have concluded that the causes of transvestism and transsexualism remain largely unknown. But the fact that we cannot fully explain the origins of transvestism or secondary transsexualism does not mean that a comprehensive theory is impossible. Indeed, excellent theoretical statements have been proposed concerning each of these topics. . . .

In my reading of the clinical literature and CD-written publications and in discussions with other CDs, I've identified nine consistently cited motivations for male cross-dressing:

1. "I was born this way."
2. Masculine failure, including:
   (a) disappointment with masculinity;
   (b) jealousy, or envy of females and female privileges,
   (c) the idealization of femininity
3. A heightened sense of aesthetic and tactile response (often falsely characterized as fetishism)
4. "Cross-dressing makes me feel good."
5. Childhood humiliation involving women's clothing
6. "I'm a woman who was born in a man's body."
7. "I was a woman in a past life."

8. Cross-dressing as part of another sexual avenue
9. "I have an irresistible urge to dress like a woman. I can neither understand nor control it."

Let's examine each of these nine motivations:

1. *"I was born this way."* This is the leading cause cited by CDs. They say that an innate desire to wear women's clothing was present in early childhood (age two to five). What does such a childhood desire indicate? It could signify an issue in a boy's relationship to his mother, or it might suggest that embryonic conditions play a role in cross-dressing. I want to leave the issue of mother for the final chapter as I believe that it has some possibilities that are better discussed in a summary context.

In terms of embryonic conditions, *Newsweek* reported in its March 27, 1995, issue on research by UCLA neuroendrocrinologists Roger Gorski and Laura Allen that indicated there are distinct differences in the corpus callosum of male and female brains. The article mentioned that other researchers have identified differences in the temporal lobe and anterior commisure regions of the brain. If differences in brain structure, or what is called *brain dimorphism*, ultimately account for the differences between men and women, then there is a possibility that the CD possesses feminine tendencies due to an altered, or feminized, brain structure.

It is well known that we all begin life at conception as "females." Chromosomes carried by the sperm and hormonal activity in the womb trigger the embryo to become male. Given that our common condition at conception is female, the possibility exists that problems can occur during the hormonal transition to the male stage. Anatomical hermaphroditism, though rare, is such a transitional problem.

Hermaphroditism is a biological quirk in which the chromosomes that trigger the fetus to become male are somehow scrambled, causing the fetus to develop genital characteristics of both sexes. It is not unreasonable to speculate that a much more subtle glitch could occur within the development of the fetal brain of the CD. John Money and Patricia Allen suggested in their 1975 book, *Sexual Signatures*, that if a male embryo were exposed to excess levels of female hormones during a critical phase of brain development, a boy with feminine tendencies and/or feminine physical features could result.

If such feminizing activity occurred only in the brain, the effects would be manifested psychologically rather than physically. Such a form of brain-hermaphroditism, if you will, would express itself in a male as a predisposition to identify with femininity. This identification would naturally be in conflict with the parental and cultural expectations for the boy to be masculine.

Brain-hermaphroditism, if it does exist, might be analogous to dyslexia in that it would cause a male to "see" his sex backward. Like dyslexia a hundred years ago, brain-hermaphroditism would be undetectable, and so its symptoms would be diagnosed as some other condition, particularly if a society were prone to view such a condition as immoral or perverse.

A person born with dyslexia a hundred years ago might well have been called stupid. He would have grown up believing that he was stupid and accepting the status accorded to the weak of mind. He would have been denied an education, job training, and other privileges of the intelligent. He might not have realized any of his inherent potential because he created a self-image based upon what culture told him about himself. His inner life would have been a dialogue about how unfortunate it was to have been born stupid. His daily life would have been arranged around his disability.

And so it might be with the CD. What if a fetal condition accounts for his behavior, yet his culture tells him that he is perverted, strange, and immoral? Absent the knowledge that he was born this way, the CD would develop a complex and troubled inner dialogue about what caused his "sexual" problem. Was it his relationship to his mother? His father? The CD would labor to build a life in spite of his seeming sexual disability.

The tendency in our culture is not to allow for sexual differences. Instead, society compares cross-dressing, for example, with "normal" heterosexuality and insists that the CD be restored to the so-called normal state if he is to be accepted. But this is like saying that all foreigners are really Americans who simply haven't realized and accepted this fact. Perhaps you can no more "cure" a cross-dresser of cross-dressing than you can cure a Canadian of being Canadian.

While science cannot currently, and may never, determine if the CD was "born that way," one danger of casually embracing a biological cause for cross-dressing is that it discourages the necessary work of self-examination. To claim that one was born a certain way can be an excuse offered by the lazy to avoid the hard work of achieving personal growth and self-insight. While this characterization fits some CDs, the majority of CDs I know are tortured with trying to solve the riddle of their cross-dressing. After years, sometimes decades, of looking for an answer, most of them simply decide, or truly realize, that they *were* born that way.

A gay researcher recently cited a difference in the size of the hypothalamus of gay men as a possibility in explaining homosexuality. Critics of the genetic view of homosexuality argue that homosexuality is a matter of choice. But is it? No one ever consciously chooses to be heterosexual, so how could one consciously choose to be homosexual? On this matter, Dr. John Money stated in his 1988 work, *Gay, Straight, and In-Between:*

> Homosexuals do not make a voluntary or intellectual decision to be erotically attracted toward, and to fall in love with, someone of the same sex. The propensity to do so is something that reveals itself, in much the same way as a dream reveals itself.

Similarly, the CD does not make a voluntary or intellectual choice to be erotically attracted to women's clothing. True, there is a choice to perform the act of cross-dressing, but this choice is one of actualizing what already exists. In the same way that each of us was a virgin until we chose to act upon our already existing sexuality by climbing into bed with another person, so, too, the CD is one who has simply acted upon those urges that have always been present within him.

Why is it so difficult for some to accept the notion that a person can be born a homosexual or a cross-dresser? One cultural barrier is presented by religious fundamentalism. If society or science were to grant, for example, that a person can be born a homosexual or a cross-dresser, then the Bible would suffer damage because it denounces these forms of behavior as immoral choices. The religious right has a vested interest in making sure that cross-dressing and homosexuality remain immoral choices so that the authority of the Bible isn't threatened.

Yet if one has no choice over his sexual orientation, then there is nothing inherently immoral about it. However, this doesn't excuse harmful behavior, for, like the person who may have been born with violent tendencies, those with harmful sexual tendencies, such as rapists or child molesters, must be identified and controlled through therapy, drugs, or incarceration.

Regardless of whether one's sexual desires are inborn or learned, the fact remains that each of us is ultimately accountable and responsible for our sexual expression. Therefore, it is the matter of personal responsibility rather than origin that is crucial in relating to one's sexual preferences.

2. *Masculine failure.* A commonly cited cause of cross-dressing is the feeling that, as a young boy, one utterly failed at masculinity. The rites of passage into masculinity can be physically and psychologically brutal for young boys, who are expected to be aggressive, athletic, competitive, physical, and confrontational. They are expected to grow up and become macho men.

But what of the sensitive or frail boys who either couldn't or wouldn't fit into the macho mold? What of the boys who wouldn't kill an animal or engage in a fistfight? They were often labeled sissies by their disappointed fathers, brothers, and peers. Boys react differently to masculine failure. Some become tyrants or overachievers; some become artists or intellectuals; and some retreat into the literal safety of mother's skirts. By this I mean that certain boys identify with femininity because they see it as safer, more nurturing, and less demanding. Naturally such boys come to be preoccupied with the feminine world. Cross-dressing becomes a natural extension of their retreat into femininity.

Three interrelated factors seem to cascade from masculine failure and contribute to cross-dressing:

1. Disappointment with masculinity
2. The idealization of femininity
3. Jealousy, or the envy of female privileges

The sequence is emotionally logical. The young boy feels himself to be a failure at masculinity and retreats into cross-dressing only to find that he's not supposed to like girlish things. He becomes disappointed that his masculine status won't allow him to be as soft, expressive, and gently clothed as girls. Masculinity becomes disappointing, for it both confirms his failure and prohibits him from obtaining the comforts of femininity.

Because femininity is something he wants and cannot have, the boy begins to idealize it. He begins to believe that femininity is a rarefied, beautiful state. Most ugly aspects in life, many insults, many problems, become associated with masculinity. The solution often seems to be femininity. So the boy starts his secret life of cross-dressing. Additionally he idolizes the beautiful women he sees in movies and on television. Unlike other boys, however, he doesn't want to marry them. Rather, he wants to be like them. He wants to look, dress, and act exactly as they do.

His idealization leads him to envy girls and women because he believes that they are accorded special privileges and luxuries. Girls get to wear pretty clothing and shoes; they aren't disciplined as harshly as boys; they don't have to work when they grow up; they get much more attention and caring than boys.

While these are generalizations, it should nevertheless be noted that siblings are vitally interested in the issue of equality. So if brother sees sister get something he doesn't, or if she is punished lightly when he receives a spanking for the same behavior, then the notion that girls have it better is justified in his mind. Such sibling jealousy is intensified when the young CD attaches the idealization of femininity to it.

From my own experience, I know that part of the joy of childhood is that excited, impatient sense of looking forward to getting something you really want; it's also about imitating a particular grownup that you like. So what happens when you discover that you'll never be able to get what you want or be like the person you admire? You become disappointed.

When I was a boy, I adored Julie Newmar. I thought that she was so beautiful and alluring. I wanted to be just like her. I wanted to look like her, dress like her, and act like her. Was it wrong for a boy to have a woman as a role model? Was it wrong for a boy to want to dress like his role model? In a cultural sense it was wrong, but I certainly didn't want to be like John Wayne, John Glenn, or any of the other macho heroes of the 1960s.

Yet I learned that not only could I never enjoy the tactile sensations of wearing girls' clothing, but I could also never get to be a pretty woman like Julie Newmar. I was stuck being a dumb, ugly boy. For me, masculinity was a big disappointment that I neither wanted nor liked. I often felt envious of girls because I thought they had it much easier in life and also got to be pretty.

3. *A heightened sense of aesthetic and tactile response.* The CD's sensual enjoyment of women's clothing is sometimes misinterpreted by society and the clinical community as fetishism. The simple fact is that men are not culturally encouraged to have either beautiful clothing or to luxuriate in the feel of clothing. Silk, nylon, and lace can feel fabulous on the skin. Unfortunately these goods are not widely used in male clothing.

A common episode reported by CDs is that of trying on mother's nylons, slips, or panties at an early age and experiencing the wonderful feel of the fabric against one's skin. This experience includes the aesthetic realization that mother's clothes are also very pretty and delicate. This is followed by an overwhelming sense of loss and disappointment when the young boy learns that he will never, ever, be able to wear such resplendent garments—and that if he does he will be punished and branded a sissy.

Thus a boy's tactile and aesthetic awareness is suddenly compromised by the superimposition of masculine failure and parental disdain. A simple, pleasurable bodily and visual sensation becomes lurid and taboo. Of course, a person is going to continue doing that which gives pleasure, and so the young CD will continue to wear the forbidden clothing in secret. His tactility is thus unnecessarily, and cruelly, recast as fetishism at this point since society has no precedent to grant males the full enjoyment of sight and touch.

Later, as the young CD matures and equates women's clothing with orgasm, his fetishism will be confirmed, for society also has no precedent for granting men eroticism in their choice of dress. Certainly women are allowed to experience eroticism when it comes to clothing, particularly lingerie, but men are not. I will argue later in the book that much of what we call fetishism, and cross-dressing for that matter, is more an irony of our flawed culture than a sexual problem.

One challenge in understanding cross-dressing is to distinguish between tactile and aesthetic response and true fetishism. Where does a man cross the line from sensuality to fetishism? The topic of fetishism is covered in chapters 3 and 9.

4. *"Cross-dressing makes me feel good."* Unless one has cross-dressed, the joys of cross-dressing are virtually impossible to communicate. Some theorists have suggested that the behavior releases endorphins in the CD. Whatever the cause, the CD finds enormous psychological comfort and sexual pleasure in this behavior.

This cause is the most subjective of all cited, and yet it is perhaps the most relevant if the behavior is to be understood. The need to feel good cannot be underestimated when one examines the motives underlying human behavior. The search for pleasure is elemental to human experience. The CD is simply a man who has found pleasure in an unconventional yet essentially harmless activity.

5. *Childhood humiliation involving women's clothing.* A young boy misbehaves. To punish him, his mother—or another dysfunctional female authority figure—makes him wear a girl's dress, shoes, and panties. The woman's thinking is that she must break the boy's horrible, masculine ways of acting and thinking. By forcibly feminizing him, she hopes to show that she is more powerful than he, and that she can wreak havoc on his nascent masculinity anytime she pleases.

While such humiliation could cause psychological injury to most young boys, certain boys might react by becoming terribly, and usually secretly, excited. In these cases, what was intended as punishment served only to awaken desire. Of course, one could argue that the excitement response is masking a deep fear of castration, and that crossdressing in general is merely an eroticized response to castration anxiety. I believe that there are more cogent theories to explain the behavior, particularly in the context of cross-dressing as a gender issue.

It is revealing to note that while enforced femininity is one of the least cited causes of cross-dressing in the clinical literature, it is the most prominent motif found within the erotic literature of crossdressing. This contrast is intriguing: Do all CDs secretly wish to be forced into femininity?

I think they do. Forced cross-dressing, to the adult CD, is a common sexual fantasy for the same reason that being sexually dominated by a woman is a fantasy to many non-cross-dressing men. In the CD's case, female clothing is involved in the fantasy because CDs like female clothing.

Also, if the CD is *forced* to cross-dress, then he's not really responsible for his feelings, is he? Forced cross-dressing lets the CD off the hook; he has to neither explain nor account for his strange feelings. Imagine it, men: Wouldn't it be wonderful if a cunning, powerful, beautiful seductress forced you to wear her silky clothing, suckle her large breasts, and then have sex? Not only would I offer no resistance, but I would look for ways to ensure my constant recapture. Is the villainess of the CD's fantasy the all-powerful Freudian woman who threatens castration only to decide at the last moment to engage in the ultimate oedipal fantasy? Perhaps.

6. *"I'm a woman who was born in a man's body."* This is the most often cited reason in the case of transsexualism. Is it even possible for a woman to be born into a man's body?

Conception is a roll of the dice. Egg and sperm meet randomly and sex is assigned on that basis. To say that one is a woman born into a male body presumes that conception is not random. A lack of randomness assumes that one existed as a sentient spirit prior to conception, and that one somehow has the power to determine his sex. If this were the case, there would then have to be an event in which a uniquely female spirit was somehow diverted into a male body either by accident or intrigue.

Metaphysically speaking, the notion that there is such a thing as a uniquely female spirit goes against the prevailing spiritual view which holds that the human spirit is both male and female. Further, this view holds that the human spirit cycles through both male and female bodies during its various incarnations. Moreover, the theory that a spirit could wind up in the wrong body would violate the immutable law of Karma, which flawlessly ensures that the reincarnational destiny of each soul is justly carried out.

Biblically speaking, the notion that a person could be born in the wrong body would be impossible, since it assumes that Jehovah, the embodiment of perfection, would make a mistake.

The logical explanation for transsexualism is the psychological, for it is easy to see how an individual might strongly identify with the opposite sex from an early age. The matter of whether such an identification is rooted in the biological realm remains open to question.

7. *"I was a woman in a past life."* Femininity sometimes feels so natural and familiar to the CD that he can't help but wonder if he was a woman in a past life. Of course, this interpretation requires that one be open to the idea of reincarnation. Not all CDs are so inclined, but for those who are, reincarnation provides a plausible explanation for their behavior. The notion that the individual is a duality of male and female energy allows us to see the CD as a spirit who, while occupying a male body, prefers to express the female energy. I personally favor this explanation since I feel so at home in the feminine role. I've also had powerful experiences which have convinced me that I have lived as a woman in previous lives.

8. *Cross-dressing as part of another sexual avenue.* Forced cross-dressing is not uncommon in the arena of bondage and discipline. It's used by dominant mistresses to degrade the masculinity of their male slaves. The real dynamic for the slave is not the cross-dressing but rather the submission to the mistress. Wearing women's clothing is understood to be an admission that the male slave's masculinity is a pathetic joke. Yet as we will see in chapter 3, the notion that it's de-

grading for a man to dress like a woman is misogynistic, for the cross-dressing seen within bondage and discipline reinforces the idea that women are inferior.

A flamboyant form of cross-dressing, called "camp," serves to exaggerate the clichés of femininity. The "Praise-the-Lord"-era Tammy Faye Baker served as a role model for some camp artists. Her bizarre use of eye shadow and false eyelashes was the envy of just about anyone who aspired to camp greatness.

There are two versions of camp. The first is the gay version. Gay camp is a celebration of masculinity, an assertion that mere femininity cannot suppress the indomitable manliness bursting forth from under the feather boa. Rather than disguise one's masculinity, gay camp is typified by the muscled, mustachioed, hirsute man wobbling on high heels and wearing a feather boa, huge torpedo breasts, and a strapless dress.

The other version of camp is seen at Mardi Gras or Carnival. This type represents the ancient tradition of role switching practiced at many pagan festivals. It is very much in the Bacchanalian tradition of grandiose costumery and decadent festivity so treasured by the hedonistic and so reviled by the unimaginative and sober.

9. *"I have an irresistible urge to dress like a woman. I can neither understand nor control it."* This statement is usually found underneath most of the other motives we've discussed. I can relate to this reason, and I think my experience echoes that of other CDs. Though I've done much soul-searching, I've never discovered the exact reason why I enjoy cross-dressing. Sometimes I think I understand myself, and other times I find that I have no understanding whatever concerning my behavior.

I tried unsuccessfully to quit cross-dressing when I was a young man contemplating entering the ministry. But I couldn't quit, not even for God. I don't even try to kid myself anymore; I could no more give up cross-dressing than I could voluntarily refrain from breathing. I stopped asking questions a long time ago. While this book is a reflection of my past questioning, the only resolution or answer I offer to other CDs is that of utter self-acceptance.

Cross-dressing often reminds me of the old *Star Trek* episode in which Mr. Spock gets the seven-year-Vulcan-mating-itch. Suddenly the hyperrationality of Spock is vaporized in a hormonal cloud of Vulcan lust. He begins to act in strange ways that the crew of the starship *Enterprise* cannot fathom.

Cross-dressing can be very much like this. A perfectly sane, successful businessman, for example, can find himself inventing all sorts of reasons to go on an overnight business trip when the urge hits. There is no arguing with the urge, for it is both incomprehensible and irresistible. The businessman's only response can be to make reservations at the Sheraton.

Is this compulsive? Yes, it is. Is this compulsion something to worry about? Not necessarily, for just as Spock recovered from his frenzy in time to save the Enterprise from ruin, the businessman will find himself back at work the morning following an enjoyable evening of cross-dressing. After all, the businessman is not completely irrational: A guy has got to work hard the next day to justify the cost of an evening out of town at the Sheraton.

CROSS-DRESSING IN AN ELECTION YEAR

Knowing the main motivations for male cross-dressing hardly scratches the surface of this fascinating topic. In the following chapters we will meet eleven different types of CDs in order to see how the motives we've outlined are expressed in the lives of individuals.

As we will learn, most cross-dressing goes on behind closed doors or in private clubs. Despite the clouds of secrecy in which cross-dressing is shrouded, I often amuse myself by imagining what the world would be like if cross-dressing played an important role in current affairs.

During the 1992 election, I found myself thinking how much more fun the presidential campaign would be if the candidates were seeking the CD vote. Accordingly I penned the following fantasy in the September 1992 edition of "The TV Social Register." The column opened by mentioning the PPOC Trailer Rancho, which itself was a fabrication that took on a life of its own:

CROSS-DRESSING AND ELECTORAL VOTES

Bad news for the investors who have shoveled money into the PPOC Trailer Rancho! The project has been halted midway through construction due to pressure from a conservative parents' group. The group, Parents Against Nudists, Transvestites, and the Institutionalized Encouragement of Sexuality, has filed a motion to delay the project with the Orange County, California, zoning board, citing a danger to "community values."

"We can't have a bunch of godless cross-dressers flaunting their perversion by cavorting about in a trailer park while dressed in womanly attire. Why, if we let them build that trailer park who knows where they'll stop! Maybe they won't be happy until the whole world wears garter belts!" complained Benjamin Fino, president of the parents' group. The zoning board placed a thirty-day moratorium on the project pending further study.

This incident immediately became a cause célèbre, for now it seems that cross-dressing has been fanned into an election year issue. Presidential candidate Bill Clinton vowed to go on the Arsenio Hall show once again—only this time he will appear in a dress, wig, and high heels. "I want to show my support for the cross-dressing community," Clinton remarked. "Both Hillary and I feel that people should be allowed to wear whatever they please."

Not to be outdone in an election year, President Bush, speaking from Dulles International Airport, said that he had dispatched Dan Quayle *en femme* to perform at the Queen Mary, a nightclub in Studio City, California, that features a female impersonation show.

"The Republican Party won't be happy until Dan, or rather, Danielle, has had her sex change," vowed Bush. "Never let it be said that we can't put on a dress and lipstick just like the next guy!" the president insisted as he boarded *Air Force One* for what he called a "TV party in the Poconos."

Perennial presidential hopeful and Democratic Party gadfly Jerry Brown accused Bush and Clinton of "inauthentic and cynical transvestism." He continued his attack by arguing, "This is just a play for votes with them, for neither Bush nor Clinton is a true cross-dresser as I am." To buttress his point, Brown produced a photograph of himself at a 1958 Jesuit drag ball. Dressed as Joan of Arc, Brown is seen in the photograph leading captive a dog-collared group of what appear to be nervous, naked, perspiring seminarians.

All of this has caused quite a backlash among the religious right, who are now deriding what they call the "bra and panty" vote. "Sure, cross-dressers are a big voting bloc, but they'll not succeed," warned Natalie Hand, director of Operation Drag Rescue, a militant Christian group that has been known to kidnap transvestites. Drag Rescue attempts to deprogram transvestites by forcing them to repeatedly listen to Reverend Kenneth Copeland's "The Godly Man" tape series. Reverend Copeland could not be reached for comment.

2

ELEVEN DIFFERENT TYPES OF CROSS-DRESSERS

During my final year of high school, all of the senior class had to take a career assessment test. During my three-minute follow-up interview, the career counselor told me that my test indicated that I would do well in a job in which I worked with people. Unfortunately time did not allow her to be any more specific. I was left wondering if "working with people" meant that I should be a hairdresser, a Las Vegas–style hypnotist, or the militant dictator of a large country.

Minorities complain that such assessment tests are biased. They don't know the half of it. I've yet to take a single assessment test that asked if I was a cross-dresser. Further, if such a test question did exist, the test would undoubtedly assume that all CDs were alike. When the CD checked *yes* next to the question "Are you a cross-dresser?" the computer would automatically default to those careers that the test-writers felt CDs would be good at—and what stereotypical careers would those be? Women's underwear buyer? Pantyhose tester? Or perhaps female impersonator in a drag revue?

After graduation, each new CD embarks upon a different transvestic career. Some become West Hollywood drag queens, others stay in the closet and work for the post office, while some travel from talk show to talk show talking about the topic of transvestism. It is important to know about the many different types of CDs, if for no other reason than you may find yourself seated next to one of us on an airliner. And at such a time wouldn't it be nice to know the difference between a fetishist and a transsexual?

Cross-dressing has become a very hip subject, and knowledge of it is considered chic. Armed with insight into matters transvestic, you might be mistaken for a psychiatrist or even an intimate of the late law enforcement eonist, J. Edgar Hoover, who, by the way, went by the name Muriel, if one is to believe an aged CD who claims to have occasionally partied with the cross-dressed Hoover in a suite of a fashionable New York hotel. That J. Edgar went by the name Muriel is in doubt; that he was capable of enjoying himself at a party is almost impossible to believe.

In any event, I will begin this part of your tutorial by dividing CDs into four main types and eleven subtypes. Are there additional types? Probably. But to develop a list that would please everybody would require a level of tedium equal to the Discovery Channel's latest program on the invention of the hinge. Here is my Table of Transvestism:

THE TABLE OF TRANSVESTISM

The Peripheral CD	*The Fetishistic CD*
The Slave	The Fetishist
The Exhibitionist	The Transitional Fetishist
The Female Impersonator	The Drag Queen

The Cosmetic CD	*The Full-Time CD*
The Closet CD	The Transgenderist
The Social CD	The Transsexual (Pre- and Post-
The She Male	operative)

What makes these categories distinctive? The yardstick I used to arrive at my groupings is the degree of emotional need to express an inner feminine self. For example, the first category in cross-dressing is composed of those men I call *peripheral CDs*. Unlike other CDs, the peripheral CD is not sexually excited by women's clothing, nor does he cross-dress in order to express an inner feminine self. Rather, the peripheral CD uses women's clothing as a means to an end.

An example of a peripheral CD would be a female impersonator. A female impersonator is usually a gay man who dresses as a woman for the sake of performance; he has no sense of an interior feminine self. While he may refer to himself as being feminine, this is but gay-speak for emotional and sexual submissiveness. The gay female impersonator ultimately wishes to remain a man and to relate to other men sexually.

Aside from the remarkably convincing female appearance that is achieved by some female impersonators, there is little that is psychologically fascinating about them. As soon as they remove their makeup, they go back to being men. Indeed, female impersonators do not take female hormones. Typically they are men who were born with feminine features.

In those instances where such performers have breast implants, take female hormones, and live full time in the role of women, I cease to define them as female impersonators and instead classify them as either drag queens or transsexuals. Such fine distinctions as these will be made where needed throughout the book.

The second category of CD is *fetishistic*. A fetishist, except in the case of a drag queen, seldom dresses fully as a woman. In this sense, he is not truly a CD. Sexual fetishism, as it applies to women's clothing, is defined as a compulsion to masturbate with a given article of apparel. The fetishist is thus motivated by a psychosexual fascination rather than a need to express an inner feminine self. The fetishist is said to be unconsciously seeking an emotional connection with a particular woman, typically his mother or a girlfriend. He establishes this connection through her clothing, which he uses to symbolize her.

The third of my four categories is composed of those men who have a decided psychological need to express their femininity. This class of CD expresses his need primarily in cosmetic terms. The *cosmetic CD*, as I call him, does not want to be a woman; he simply enjoys being feminine, or womanlike, on an occasional basis, typically between two and eight times per month. The cosmetic CD has an inner feminine self. He feels that this distinct part of his personality needs to be expressed.

The cosmetic CD enjoys femininity and all of its artifacts such as cosmetics, clothing, jewelry, high heels, and painted fingernails. This type of CD dresses fully as a woman, including a wig, and sometimes shaves his body hair to achieve a more realistic feminine appearance. He will also adopt feminine mannerisms when he dresses. Most men in this category are married heterosexuals who think of themselves as men who like to dress as women.

The final category of CD includes those who see themselves as women. Their inner feminine self has a much greater reality and permanence than the male self into which they are born. *Full-time CDs* are not chiefly interested in the cosmetic aspects of femininity. Rather, they choose to adopt a full-time feminine role in life. Accordingly, they do not consider themselves to be "cross-dressing" when they wear women's clothing, for their choice of clothing is said to reflect an inner reality. Accordingly, many of the CDs in this group take female hormones to feminize their bodies, hence the term *chemical CD* can be used to speak of them. These hormones exert an additional influence upon the psyche that is often described as feminine in nature.

Some *transgenderists,* who live full time in the gender role that society considers appropriate to the opposite sex, argue that they represent a third gender that exists in the gray area between male and female. The male-to-female transsexual, however, does not consider himself a member of a third gender. Rather, he believes that he is a woman who was born with a birth defect—namely, male genitals.

THE EVOLUTION OF THE CROSS-DRESSER

I think of the CD population in terms of a pyramid. I suspect that there are a great number of anonymous, fetishistic men in the world who do not dress completely as women. Instead, they enjoy wearing only one or two articles of women's clothing, particularly panties and bras. However, many of these men progress beyond panties and bras and begin to dress completely as women on an occasional basis. A few of these CDs go beyond occasional cross-dressing and start to live as women on a full-time basis. At the apex of the pyramid dwell those full-time CDs who have elected to have sexual reassignment surgery.

I can't prove my pyramid statistically. I'm not an academician with a research staff, and I don't care to stand in front of Home Depot with a clipboard and ask men if they wear women's underwear or practice other forms of cross-dressing. The lack of statistics is part of the problem in discussing cross-dressing in general. The valuable statistical work that has been done by Dr. Docter and other mental health professionals generally measures only those CDs who are associated with support groups and is therefore somewhat skewed.

The problem of statistics aside, what makes the pyramidal view intriguing are the questions of why and how. Why do men express cross-dressing in so many different ways? Why are there so many fetishists and so few transsexuals? How do transsexuals get to the point where they decide to have their male genitals surgically removed?

Within transvestic evolution is a progressively more intense search to find and express one's feminine self. But is it truly a search to find one's feminine self? Or could it be that there is actually an unconscious search to find something else and express that something through one's own self? To answer the riddle of cross-dressing requires that we take a most unusual journey through the worlds of cross-dressing, culture, fetishism, sexual dysfunction, and spirituality.

The best route on our grand tour of cross-dressing is to begin from the male periphery and work our way along the winding road until we arrive in the feminine heartland. By following this path, the evolutionary ascent of cross-dressing will become evident.

THE FEMALE IMPERSONATOR AND THE DRAG QUEEN

The most visible members of the CD community, the drag queen and the female impersonator, provide a useful contrast between the peripheral CD and the fetishistic CD. People always confuse that celebrated diva of the stage, the female impersonator, with her star-crossed cousin, the drag queen. While they both dress as women, they are quite different.

Female impersonators, as we mentioned, are men who dress as women only for the sake of performance; they do not dress like women offstage. Robin Williams as Mrs. Doubtfire is a recent example of a cinematic female impersonator. We know from confirmed Robin Williams sightings throughout the land that this man does not dress as a woman offstage. Further, though Mr. Williams is not gay, the majority of men who earn their living as female impersonators are.

As a style of costume, the term *drag* can be used to denote a distinctive, highly fetishistic interpretation of femininity. While the female impersonator may dress in "drag," he is not truly a drag queen as I use the term. This same distinction also applies to gay men who flamboyantly dress as women for festive purposes. Such dressing is better termed *camp* than *drag*. However, because the connotations of the term *drag* are considered more chic than those of *camp*, the drag label is appropriated.

Motivation is the key difference between the female impersonator and the drag queen. I class the female impersonator as a peripheral CD because he has no real need to experience femininity nor does he gain any sexual excitement from dressing or acting like a woman. The drag queen, on the other hand, is a true cross-dresser in that he has a psychological need to cross-dress, and this need is expressed in fetishistic terms.

Drag queens are a walking example of fetishism: Stiletto heels, fishnet stockings, miniskirts, and the heavy use of cosmetics typify this genre of cross-dressing. Due to this fetishistic emphasis, the drag queen is markedly different from the cosmetic CD, who generally opts for a more realistic interpretation of feminine dress. Unlike the closeted fetishist who wears only women's underwear, the drag queen represents an escalation of fetishism from a single object into an expression of an inner feminine self.

In terms of a generalized personality sketch, I would say that drag queens have a hostile attitude strikingly similar to that often seen among prostitutes, certain gay men, and other sexual minorities. Their hostility seems to be one born of their overwhelming sexual desires, powerful and uncontrollable negative emotions—typically self-hatred—and a pronounced cynicism directed at an unaccepting and critical world. Drag queens also frequently exhibit a history of sexual abuse and a predisposition toward substance abuse.

Drag queens are infamous for their jaded worldliness. They are typically characterized as sexual libertines, and many seem to seek to create scandal through promiscuous and obscene behavior. To the trained eye, such gestures are not shocking; instead, they are understood as behaviors requiring therapy. However, a person who will "fuck and suck" anybody shocks most people—especially if that person is a flamboyantly attired drag queen who is after other men.

It is not surprising that prostitution is so often associated with drag queens, for many of them lead a life that leaves few options for normal employment. The stereotype of the drag queen working the boulevard next to the "real girls" exists for a good reason, namely that transvestite prostitution is a fact of life in any large city. Not all drag queens are prostitutes, but enough of them do work in this oldest of professions to merit the stereotype.

Many drag queens are drug addicts who get dressed up like street whores and turn a few tricks to earn money to support their habits. They find it an exciting, erotic lifestyle when they're high. Not unexpectedly, AIDS has taken a serious toll on the drag community.

A drag queen I know is dying of AIDS. She believes that her choice to follow her sexual urges and become a drag queen made her begin taking drugs. "I started taking drugs because I felt so screwed up about cross-dressing and having sex with men," she declared. This complaint has been echoed by other CDs who have faced substance abuse problems; many men can enjoy their guilty cross-dressing only when they're under the influence.

Substance abuse and cross-dressing are a dangerous combination. Substance abuse is by no means unique to drag queens; it's only more noticeable because of their lifestyle. The topic of cross-dressing and substance abuse will be discussed in chapter 7 when we explore the "Black Lace Prison."

One of the attractive features of drag is its perverse sense of humor. *Dragazine,* a Los Angeles–based magazine devoted to the world of drag, is published by a drag queen (though I'm not sure I would call her that) who goes by the name of Lois Commondemoninator. *Dragazine*, like its publisher, is thoroughly enjoyable. The magazine is devoted to photographs, fashion, gossip, interviews with noted female impersonators and drag queens, and reporting on others who hang around the scene. A sample of Lois's thoughts from the "Media Notes" section of the hard-to-find number 4 issue:

" 'Drag?' I'm offended by the term!" At least that's what Holly Woodlawn said to cable maven Skip E. Lowe on local Access. Holly— you're a Drag Queen, I'm a Drag Queen, we're *all* Drag Queens, so get over it, girl! Dateline (I love saying that!) Colombia—*Los Angeles Times* of 7/2/92 reports that drug lord Pablo Escobar escaped from prison by wearing jeans, a sweater, and a wig to fool the Colombian army guards during a confusing fracas. One of five things might be true—either the guards were blind, paid off, dumb, into Drag Queens, or Pablo should be doing makeovers in Beverly Hills! Locally, the *L.A. Times* is now my official Drag News Bible. A recent story on news fashions reported from the field, "Women don't come in asking to try on that shoe. Drag queens do." American Rag on La Brea Avenue here in Los Angeles had some pretty trendy platform shoes that made pulses pulsate from Pump Passion . . .

Lois Commondenominator could be right: We might all well be drag queens. For better or worse, it's that damn inhibitory network in the brain that keeps most of us from experiencing the depths of "Pump Passion." I know. I have regrets, too—but what can readily be done about such inhibitions?

A NIGHT IN THE LIFE

Shantel is a drag queen. Shantel sings and dances onstage four nights a week in stunning evening gowns, bikini bathing suits, nurses' uniforms, and many other female costumes at a nightclub that features female impersonators. Shantel has a gorgeous set of 36D breasts, luscious round hips and derriere, and beautiful full lips and cheeks, all of which come courtesy of silicone and black-market female hormones.

Unlike most drag queens, Shantel lives as a woman full time. This is somewhat unusual, for drag queens, like vampires, usually appear only at night. Despite her living full time as a woman, however, I class Shantel in the fetishistic category for several reasons. First, her style of dress is highly fetishistic: Spike heels, gartered stockings, push-up bras, miniskirts, and see-through blouses comprise her usual wardrobe.

Second, Shantel is clearly not a transsexual. Although she talks about it, she has no intention of ever having sexual reassignment surgery. That Shantel has breast implants and takes female hormones might cause some to think of her as a transsexual, but this is simply not the case, for Shantel does not consider herself to be a woman. Instead, she sees herself as an effeminate man who prefers to assume the role of a woman—particularly in a sexual relationship with a man. Further, she only takes female hormones periodically as she doesn't want to lose the ability to maintain an erection or to ejaculate.

Shantel lives with her boyfriend, Keith. Their common passions are smoking rock cocaine and having sex. Shantel turns the occasional trick when Keith, her sometimes pimp, lines up a john who wants something exotic.

It is the closing number of a packed Friday night performance. Shantel, who is dressed in a porn version of a police uniform, and the rest of the troupe of drag queens and female impersonators who perform at this club have fanned out into the audience during a big dance number. For the most part the crowd is receptive, but when the performers get too close, some become decidedly uncomfortable.

"Get away from me, you fuckin' drag queen!" yells a drunken businessman in the audience when Shantel brushes provocatively against him. One of the businessman's companions, an attractive, loud woman in her thirties, teases him about "being hit on by a chick with a dick." His mood turns ugly.

"She really likes you," the loud woman continues. "In fact, I bet she really wants to fuck you!" The whole table explodes with laughter at the thought of their masculine friend being sodomized by a drag queen. Disgusted, the man tells his friends to "fuck off." Grabbing his jacket, he gets up and exits the club to have a cigarette.

Shantel spots a single man who is looking at her with lust in his eyes. He is wearing a silk jacket and sporting a Rolex. She sits on his lap, where she can feel an obvious erection. Entranced, the man slides a ten-dollar bill into her cleavage. "I want to be with you," he whispers in her ear. She slides her index finger upward along his throat to his chin and whispers for him to meet her in the parking lot after the show. She then winks at him and moves back into the dance number.

Outside the club, while the drunken businessman smokes, a strapping fellow paces back and forth. It is Robbie, the boyfriend of Genet, one of the female impersonators who works in the show. Robbie waits every night for Genet to finish work. He has a reputation for being very jealous and possessive. Genet is a gay man and has no particular desire to dress as a woman offstage, nor has he had any surgical alterations, such as breast implants, to further feminize his appearance.

Female impersonators constitute a small, celebrated minority within the gay community. Nevertheless, it *is* the gay community, and *maleness* is what is valued. While Robbie likes effeminate men, he does not care for cross-dressed men. "If I wanted a queen, I would date someone like Shantel," Robbie once told Genet. Thus, after each show Genet turns into Robbie's lover, the effeminate Michael.

Michael first dressed as a woman for a gay ball when he was eighteen. His slender frame and delicate features made him striking. He started appearing at gay beauty contests that feature men dressed as women. After being discovered at one such contest by the owner of a drag club, he was soon onstage performing professionally. Michael got into female impersonation because it pays the bills and he enjoys performing. His real hope is to make it as a male dancer or actor. While he has performed as a male actor in Los Angeles and Las Vegas shows, female impersonation has remained his bread and butter.

After the show, Shantel and Keith meet the man in the silk jacket in the parking lot. Keith negotiates while Shantel smokes. The businessman is particularly interested in determining whether or not hormones have diminished Shantel's ability to develop an erection. Keith assures him that Shantel can get a decent erection. An agreement is reached and Shantel leaves with the businessman in his car. The businessman, as it turns out, enjoys going down on drag queens—but only if they can get it up!

After about twenty minutes, Shantel and the businessman return to the parking lot. Shantel gives the businessman a quick kiss on the cheek and exits the car. Keith and Shantel then get in their car and head out on the boulevard to score some rock cocaine.

Later, after they've smoked and had sex, Shantel tells Keith that she is worried that the illegal Mexican hormones she is taking are harming her. She complains of back pains and loss of appetite. Taking illicit female hormones without being under a doctor's supervision is yet another risk some CDs choose, as is the practice of receiving nonmedically approved injections of automotive-grade silicone to feminize the bodily contours of the lips, cheeks, hips, and buttocks. Such forms of *pirate transsexualism* abound within the sexual underground because unethical doctors and other unscrupulous characters are out to make a fast buck from CDs' desperate need to feminize themselves.

Meanwhile, Genet has finished changing back into Michael in the club's dressing room. He meets Robbie in the parking lot and they go to an after-hours gay nightclub for a drink and to meet some friends. At the club, Michael tells his friends about an audition next week for a sitcom pilot that he hopes will be his big break. "Drag is such a drag," Michael says, repeating an old cliché of the profession. "I hope this audition works out so I can hang up my heels."

Shantel and Michael are contrasting CDs whose only similarity is their appearance onstage. Shantel has been cross-dressing since she was quite young. She needs to dress and live as a woman, and she derives pleasure from wearing women's clothing and taking the passive role during sex with her boyfriend. Shantel doesn't want to have sexual reassignment surgery because she's afraid that she'll regret it.

For Michael, female impersonation is simply a means to an end. He isn't sexually aroused by women's clothing; rather, he is aroused by other men. Michael is a peripheral CD while Shantel is a drag queen. Both of these types happen to converge upon the stage, only to go their respective ways after the lights go down.

THE GAY AND CD COMMUNITIES

While some CDs, like Shantel, are gay, and others are bisexual, most CDs are heterosexual. Each of these groups tend to stay in their own communities. How does the CD community relate to the gay community?

To use a somewhat antique analogy, the difference is that of Russian communism and Chinese communism: Both are communist, but they really don't socialize much. Gay men and heterosexual CDs go to different nightclubs, read different magazines, and have different sexual needs. There are some cross-over nightclubs, like Peanuts in West Hollywood, but such clubs are really oriented more toward drag queens than cosmetic CDs.

Does this mean that the two groups don't like each other? Absolutely not. The CD community has long recognized that it stands on the shoulders of the gay community. Had it not been for the courage of gay activists from Stonewall on, CDs would not have the relative social freedom they now enjoy as a sexual minority. An element of the cross-dressing world is active in the gay community and supports its causes. Likewise, the gay community has always opened its door to CDs.

Yet what gay men want is other gay men—not men who look like women. Hence, while they are always welcome, heterosexual CDs are of little interest in the gay world. Gay men are also welcome in the CDs' world, but they attract little attention because the emphasis here is on cross-dressing.

CDs also enjoy a welcome in the lesbian community. I've always found lesbian bars to be friendly. In fact, to be dressed like a woman alongside some of the women who are dressed like men is a fascinating experience in gender-bending. Indeed, one of the more interesting experiences of my cross-dressing career occurred one night in a lesbian bar in North Hollywood.

I arrived around 10 P.M. with my friend Trish and sat down at the bar to have a drink. I noticed some women playing pool. One of them turned around, and I immediately recognized her as an old high school teacher of mine! Small world, I thought, as I walked over to reintroduce myself. We laughed and hugged. One nice thing about being in a sexual minority is that you have a certain bond with members of other sexual minorities. I'll never forget how nice it was to see my old teacher or the unusual circumstances under which we met. Still, it's an anecdote I didn't get around to sharing at my twentieth high school reunion.

THE EXHIBITIONIST

There is a strange class of men who cross-dress only for the shock value they derive from it. While such men may have begun cross-dressing as a result of fetishism or curiosity, they soon found their biggest thrill came from the shock on other people's faces. These men are nothing more than exhibitionists whose medium is women's clothing. How do such men exhibit themselves?

A family with young children is seated for lunch at the food court of a mall in upstate New York. Suddenly there is a commotion. All heads turn to behold an individual traipsing through the center of the mall. It is a CD. But it is not just any CD, it is an exhibitionistic CD. He is dressed in a short, yellow-and-black checkerboard miniskirt, and beneath the hem protrudes the crotch of his pantyhose. He is wearing a yellow Lycra leotard. From its neckline peek the tops of his foam breast pads. He shaved his chest this morning, and it is broken out.

The man's makeup looks thick, gloppy, and inexpertly applied. Blue eye shadow competes with a sickly violet hue of lipstick. Both are offset by bright red blush and a clownish, brown lipliner. His blond wig is matted on one side and badly in need of styling. Worse, his six-foot frame is boosted four inches by the black spike heels he is wearing. This man is the junky car driving too slowly on the autobahn of cross-dressing, a fashion embarrassment happening in slow motion.

The father, angry that his kids have to see such a disgusting spectacle, stifles the urge to punch the CD. Instead, he calls the mall security supervisor and asks her to have the CD removed. The security supervisor isn't sure if she has a legal right to do so. Fearing a possible lawsuit, she calls the mall manager, who in turn calls the police.

Meanwhile, the CD has made it into a ladies' shoe store. There he asks the salesgirls if he can try on some shoes. One of the teenage girls who works at the store is openly laughing at the man, telling him how ridiculous he looks, while the other two girls have become terrified and run into the back room to call mall security.

This is just what the exhibitionist CD wants, for he cross-dresses only to evoke a reaction in others. This type of pest, long considered an embarrassing nuisance by the CD community, insists that he is a CD, but his behavior and dress suggest otherwise. He is never passable as a woman when he appears in public. Instead, he dresses in ridiculous outfits designed to attract attention. To worsen matters, the more people laugh, snicker, and hurl insults, the more this fellow is emboldened to continue his pathetic exhibitionism.

A policeman and the manager of the mall show up at the shoe store. The policeman decides that the CD is harassing the employees and orders him to leave the mall or face arrest for disturbing the peace. By this time, a small crowd has gathered. The CD is eating up all of the attention. It is still early in the afternoon; he can easily make it to another mall or two before sundown.

Femininity is the last thing on this grotesque individual's mind. Still, we should be glad that he has the outlet of female clothing, for if he didn't he might well be exhibiting his penis to his involuntary audience. The father in the food court, by the way, verbally assaults the CD as he is leaving the mall by yelling, "You perverted weirdo, you oughta be in an institution!" The exhibitionist smiles and waves at the angry man.

THE SLAVE

Another type of peripheral CD is the man who wears women's clothing only within the arena of bondage and discipline. There, a mistress might well "force" a man to wear a garter belt and stockings, or other articles of female clothing, in order to humiliate him. "No, please, Mistress, please don't make me wear those panties," the slave might plead before receiving a welt-inducing whack (mistresses don't fool around with the paddle!) on his bare buttocks. Most slaves are sexually aroused by this because it caters to a fetishistic element in them and, more important, they have a need to be humiliated by a woman.

Mistress Andrea, a real woman, makes her living as a dominatrix who specializes in cross-dressing. She advertises in sexually oriented newspapers and either has men come to the converted warehouse in which she plies her trade or she goes to their homes or motel rooms.

What do men pay Mistress Andrea to do? They want her to "force" them to cross-dress and then tie, spank, and verbally humiliate them for being weak. After this, she allows them to masturbate, usually while they kneel and kiss her spike-heeled boots. Sometimes she straps on a dildo and makes them perform mock-fellatio on her. Yet other times she will make a male submissive insert a tampon into his rectum to humiliate him.

She never has sex with a client. "It breeds disrespect in a submissive," she informs me. An hour session with Andrea costs $75 to $150 depending upon the complexity and props required.

What is a typical session with Mistress Andrea like? I sat in on a session one day while dressed as her transvestite assistant. She insisted that I work as a sort of junior-dominatrix to capture, if you will, the essence of the experience.

Before a client arrives at her warehouse-cum-dungeon, Andrea always sets the stage. The room she works in is furnished in an industrial motif. The concrete walls and ceiling are unpainted. Eyebolts mounted at various elevations are conspicuous on each of the walls. The bare, rusting pipes of the fire sprinkler system etch the bare ceiling. The concrete floor is painted flat black.

A small, plush, dark gray area rug lies in the middle of the floor. Above the center of the rug hangs a white rope that is looped through an eyebolt in the ceiling. There are three 1950s-era wooden office chairs, a table covered with a black velvet tablecloth, and a black stereo speaker in each corner. The room's stark minimalism heightens the dark, serious business of bondage that goes on here.

Andrea goes into another room and puts on a compact disk of the Cocteau Twins, lights some musk incense, and dims the track lights that provide the only illumination. She next lays out several items on the table, like a doctor preparing for surgery. There are three leather paddles of differing sizes; a riding crop; a coil of white rope; an eight-inch dildo; a tube of KY jelly; one tampon; three pairs of lace panties in different colors; a pink lace bra, size 40D; a pack of cigarettes; three amyl nitrate "poppers"; a ball gag; a pair of chrome handcuffs; a bottle of Absolut vodka; three shot glasses; and an ashtray.

Andrea, by the way, hates being called a prostitute. "I'm a professional dominatrix who offers a valuable form of psychodrama to my clients," she insists. Pausing for a moment, her face changes to a severe expression and she adds, "You better not call me a prostitute in your book, or I'll bust your balls with my riding crop! Do you understand?" I nod yes, fearing to hazard my testicles for such an indiscretion.

The client, a fortyish man named Cliff, arrives punctually at four in the afternoon. He is a ruggedly handsome man whom you'd never suspect of having such exotic cravings. Andrea gives him a kiss as he enters the room. Per the established protocol of Mistress Andrea's emporium of delicious pain, Cliff pays her $100 before services are rendered.

The session begins with Andrea clad in a shiny black vinyl corset whose eight garters hold up a pair of black fishnet stockings. A pair of black lace panties, black suede spike-heeled boots, and black wrap-around sunglasses complete this fashionable bondage ensemble. She has drawn her long raven hair into a topknot. Her pierced nipples, heavy with gold and silver hoop rings, protrude through holes in the bra portion of the corset.

Andrea orders Cliff to strip. Cliff stammers and explains that he does not wish to do so today. Infuriated, Andrea grabs a paddle and whacks him on the ass. Backing away from her, Cliff asks her to calm down. This only makes Andrea more irate. "God damn it! I will not have a piece-of-shit slave telling me what he will and won't do! Now take your fucking clothes off!" she commands as she lets him have it with the paddle again.

Cliff quickly disrobes. Mistress Andrea orders him to kneel, which he does immediately. She then takes the rope that is looped through the overhead eyebolt and ties Cliff's wrists together. Pulling the rope so that his hands are raised above his head, she secures the rope to an eyebolt on the wall. She next affixes a ball gag in Cliff's mouth and ties the two ends behind his head. She then binds his feet together and blindfolds him.

Taking paddle in hand, she begins to slowly circle the kneeling man. Lighting a long, white cigarette, she grabs Cliff's hair. "You fucking sissy," she scowls as she exhales the smoke into his face. She suddenly swings her paddle with great force, striking the man's ass with a resounding crack. "You pathetic, fucking little sissy boy!" she screams as she lets loose with another swat. The man shudders and inhales deeply but says nothing.

Andrea looks over at me and says, "Cliff's problem is that he's such a goddamn wimp. I mean, he is the real fucking thing: a certifiable mama's boy, a real fucking sissy boy." With that she lets loose with another whack. Cliff's ass is now starting to take on the characteristic red glow of pain. Betraying his pleasure, Cliff is sporting quite an erection.

Andrea takes her riding crop and swats the tip of Cliff's penis. He arches back and moans in ecstasy. She continues her tirade of verbal abuse and paddling for a good fifteen minutes. She then unfastens Cliff and, removing his blindfold and gag, orders him into a prone position. As he lies prostrate on the floor, Mistress Andrea orders me to pour us drinks. I pour the Absolut and we sit down on the wooden chairs with Cliff serving as a convenient footstool.

I feel rather awkward with my heels parked on Cliff's back. Mistress Andrea all but ignores him while she sips her drink and we make small talk. She then rather nonchalantly slips off her black lace panties and slides them over Cliff's head, making sure that the crotch is situated over his nose. She orders Cliff to breathe deeply. As he does, Andrea grabs the big paddle and delivers a monumental whack on his bare buttocks. Cliff's body shudders once again.

"You fucking sissy boy," she says, scowling at him. Throwing a pair of pink lace panties and the bra at him she commands him to put them on. He stands and does as he is told. "Look at you," she sneers. "You're a little fucking faggot boy who gets off on wearing girl's panties and bras." Andrea turns to me and asks, "Justine, do you know what panty-boy Cliff secretly likes to do?"

I shake my head no.

"He likes to suck big dicks!" she answers. "And I think that's what he wants to do right now." With that, she secures the eight-inch dildo into a harness and slides the harness onto her hips. She then sits down on the chair and tells Cliff to suck her dick. Before he starts, she removes her panties from his head and breaks open an amyl nitrate popper for him. He inhales the fumes from the popper. His eyes roll back into his head momentarily.

Cliff recovers from his swoon and rather enthusiastically begins mock-fellatio on Mistress Andrea. Andrea renews her verbal humiliation of Cliff, calling him a "cock-sucking fairy" and other terms of endearment. After about five minutes, she hands Cliff another pair of panties and "orders" him to masturbate with them. He slides down the panties he is wearing and wraps the other pair around his penis. As Cliff begins to masturbate, Andrea flicks him lightly all over his body with her riding crop, all the while sustaining her verbal taunts. "You disgusting excuse for a man. You're nothing but a fucking disgusting little boy in a man's body."

As Cliff is about to climax he stops his mock-fellatio so that Mistress Andrea can give him another popper. She times the administration of the popper until Cliff yells, "Yes, yes, now," and then, at the moment of orgasm, she breaks open the popper. Cliff inhales it violently and rolls onto the floor, spasming as he spills his seed into the panties. It is all very dramatic for Cliff, I suppose, but Mistress Andrea seems unimpressed.

As Cliff is recovering from his orgasmic delirium, Mistress Andrea tells him what a good slave he is and how happy he makes her. After saying this, she turns to me, and, while stroking an imaginary penis with her hand and rolling her eyes, she stage whispers, "What a fuck this guy is!"

She then orders Cliff to pour her and me another drink. He does so in a desultory fashion, entirely to Mistress Andrea's dissatisfaction. Cliff once again incurs the stinging wrath of Mr. Paddle for his insolence.

Cliff starts to get dressed as Mistress Andrea and I sit on the wooden chairs. I ask Cliff why he does this. He replies that he needs a woman to humiliate him, and he particularly enjoys wearing her panties and bra and being spanked while being humiliated. He then mentions, surprisingly, that his wife refuses to accept or indulge his behavior.

"I asked her to do it once and she flipped. She threatened to leave me unless I got counseling," Cliff remarks dejectedly, "so I started to visit dominants. Do you think this is bizarre?" he asks me, figuring that I'm some kind of authority.

Mistress Andrea eyes me harshly, perhaps feeling that her income is about to be threatened. Thinking it best to keep my thoughts to myself for the moment, I tell Cliff, "Not at all, especially if you enjoy it. I mean, I like to dress like a woman, and I don't think there's anything bizarre about that."

What do I really think about all of this? What's bizarre about Cliff's desires is not the spanking or the humiliation per se; rather it's the way in which women's clothing is used as an instrument of humiliation. Both Mistress Andrea and Cliff share the belief that it's humiliating for a man to have to stoop to the level of being a woman, as is the case with being "forced" to wear women's clothing. The disturbing message inherent in this type of bondage is that men are superior to women, and that for a man to wear women's clothing is both degrading and humiliating.

Mistress Andrea reinforces the belief that women are inferior to men by setting herself up as the strong, smart, cruel woman who is superior to all other women because she alone can inflict pain and retribution upon men. But what is she actually doing? She's horsewhipping weak men who pay her to do so. The blows she strikes are, ironically, symbolic blows against herself and all women.

Moreover, Cliff is not a cross-dresser in any meaningful sense of the word. Instead, he is a fetishistic masochist, a man who craves pain and the humiliation of being "forced" to wear women's clothing. I don't particularly feel sorry for Cliff because I view cross-dressing as a refined, passionate, and esoteric pursuit, and he turns it into nothing more than sordid ritual. I think he's a chump who deserves to have his ass whipped by a cruel woman.

After I give my polite, albeit lying answer to Cliff, Mistress Andrea smiles approvingly and asks me, in a rather taunting fashion, if I would like a free session with her sometime so that I might be able to fully appreciate Cliff's experience. I accept her gracious offer (or was it a dare?) and take her up on it at a later date.

I did it only for the sake of literary experience; it seemed like such a *writerly* thing to do. I lasted about five minutes before wilting under the fury of the paddle. Mistress Andrea laughed and observed that I was not "a true masochist." But it's just as they've always said: If you can't stand the paddle, get out of the dungeon! It's an unusual combination, this amalgam of masochism and fetishism, yet it's one of those things that makes the mosaic of human sexuality so fascinating. Bottoms up!

3

THE REALM OF FETISHISM

A rather amusing case history from the files of Dr. Magnus Hirschfeld, the early German sexologist, is related in the 1956 book *Sexual Anomalies*. This incident probably dates from the 1920s. Although the case history is somewhat involved, the essential element, at least in my mind, is obvious:

> A woman in a divorce suit stated that, from the beginning of her marriage, her husband had expected her to wear flannelette knickers during their sexual intercourse. It was with great reluctance that she had complied, though she regarded it as a slight on herself. "Now if he had asked me to wear silk!" said the lady. "But a common material like flannelette!"

This quote illustrates one of the main problems encountered in dealing with the concept of fetishism. Apparently the woman considered silk luxurious and so would not have objected to the compulsory wearing of silk underwear. However, because she considered flannel crude, her husband's preference became fetishistic.

One of the key points of this chapter will be that what is called fetishism is often nothing more than a slur leveled against those who violate the aesthetic or symbolic sensibilities of another person or group. If the fetishist and the CD are guilty of anything, it is this violation of society's aesthetic and symbolic sense of propriety: A man who dresses like a woman is seldom attractive in the usual sense and sometimes even seems to be mocking women.

But is society's disdain for the CD valid? Should not the right of personal expression be senior to that of aesthetic and symbolic propriety? In this chapter we'll explore these questions in terms of fetishism, which I consider to be the doorway into true cross-dressing. We'll begin our journey by meeting the classic entry-level CD: the man who likes to wear women's underwear.

BOB: A MAN WITH A BIG-TIME PANTY FETISH

This is perhaps an understatement, but my friend—I'll call him Bob—has a panty fetish. He is a peripheral CD and has dressed as a woman only for Halloween. However, because he does wear women's panties, he meets the broad definition of a CD. Here's how he describes his interest:

> I've been collecting and wearing women's panties for over twenty years. At last count I had about 2,100 pairs in my collection. I know that sounds like a lot, but if you average it over twenty years it's only 102 pairs per year, or two pairs per week, so it really didn't take that much time or effort. Dollar-wise, I'd say that I've put over $8,000 into my collection.
>
> A lot of the older pairs have fallen apart because the elastic has disintegrated, but I still keep them because I can't bear the thought of throwing them away. I keep them locked in three four-drawer file cabinets in the closet of my den. My kids think there's tax records in those cabinets.
>
> I have a couple of pilfered pairs from laundromats in my collection, but those are from my younger days. I have some panties that old girlfriends gave me, but other than those few pairs, I've purchased everything else. I would never dream of stealing a pair of panties—just imagine the embarrassment of being caught! Not only would I lose my job, but my wife and kids would shoot me!
>
> I started wearing panties when I was four years old. It was after my evening bath. The phone rang and my mother left me in my towel for a few minutes to take the call. I went into her bedroom,

and for some unknown reason I slipped on a pair of her frilly panties. An indescribable feeling of happiness and warmth came over me that I'll never forget.

My mother walked in and laughed, "Well, don't you look cute. Do you want some little panties of your own?" I was so embarrassed. My mother didn't make a big deal out of it; she just took off the panties and then dressed me in my pajamas. After that I started to play with my mom's or my sister's panties whenever I could sneak a pair.

I continued to sneak either my mom's or my sister's panties. A big change occurred for me when I was twelve. My mom's girlfriend, Helen, a real fox, came over to our house on a hot summer day to do laundry because the power had gone out at her apartment building. She did her laundry and then left. My mom then washed and dried a load of our clothes. Mom had to go shopping, so she took the clothes out of the dryer and put them on the kitchen table for my sister to fold later. This left me by myself in the house for an hour.

I went over to the pile of clothes to get a pair of my sister's panties when I found *them*. Apparently a pair of Helen's panties had stuck to the inside of our clothes dryer and Mom hadn't seen them. This was a pair I was going to keep because my mom and sister didn't have any like these! They were the kind of panties that I'd always imagined sexy ladies like Helen would wear. They were baby blue bikini panties with black lace trim.

I rushed into the bathroom and put them on. While I had worn panties before, this was a magical experience because it was the first time I'd ever really been sexually turned on. As I began to fondle myself in the panties, I imagined that I was a beautiful woman with gorgeous breasts, supple skin, curved hips, and a smooth round ass. I tucked my genitals between my legs to look like a girl, but they kept sliding out from between my legs because the nylon was so slippery. I kept putting my genitals back and discovered how pleasurable it felt when they slid against the nylon. Before I knew it, I had my first orgasm. Those panties excited me in a way that I had never known, and I've loved playing with panties ever since.

That experience was so intensely pleasurable, yet I felt so tremendously guilty. I was ashamed of myself for a week afterward. Despite my shame the urge soon overtook me, and I once again found myself locked in the bathroom. This pattern of pleasure and guilt characterized my life until I met my wife in college.

I told her about my panty fetish soon after we started dating. Her love and acceptance really helped me to accept this quirk in myself. Fortunately my interest doesn't bother her; at least she knows what to buy me for my birthday. Her father was a gun collector who was obsessed with his collection, so I guess the idea of an obsessive man isn't new to her. Anyway, she says she's glad that I don't force our guests to see my panty collection in the same way that her father forced everyone to go into his den to look at his gun collection.

My wife says that her only real concern is finding a nonembarrassing way to get rid of my panty collection when I die. I'm forty years old now. If I live another thirty-five years and keep collecting panties at my present rate, I'll wind up with about 5,800 pairs of panties—and she wants to know how she could explain that many panties to Goodwill.

I usually shop for panties on my lunch hour. The big department store clearance sales are the best places to buy good panties inexpensively. The only problem for a man is that you have to go elbow-to-elbow with the women customers at the clearance bins, and sometimes they are wont to make sniping remarks.

After beating her to a beautiful pair of Vanity Fair panties, I once had a woman whisper under her breath, "Panty freak." Just for fun, I gave her a demented laugh. She ran off into the dressing rooms like a scared rabbit. It wasn't the first time I've had something like that happen, but I figure, hell, it's a free country, and I can buy as many pairs of panties as I want!

I've worn panties under my male clothing ever since I got out of high school. The few times I've had to wear men's underwear to go to the doctor's or when I've been out overnight with my fishing buddies, it felt strange. I only own three pairs of men's underpants, and they must be about ten years old.

The only time I ever got caught wearing women's underwear was on a Saturday when I was out shopping for carpet. I had on a beautiful pair of floral print bikini panties that were trimmed in black lace. Now, I have some panties that are borderline, that you might not be sure if they were women's underwear if you saw them, but this pair was so undeniably feminine that it just figures that I'd be wearing them on this day.

Anyway, I had gone to this cut-rate carpet warehouse on a Saturday morning and the place was jam-packed. So I knelt down to look at a roll of carpet. I guess that I had overstressed the seat of the slacks I was wearing when I knelt, because the seat of my slacks popped open just like the tension seal on a jar of instant iced tea does when you flick it sharply with your finger.

Not only did the seat of my slacks rip wide open, but they made a loud, abrupt crack as they did so. People looked over, and, just for a minute as I stood there frozen in embarrassment, I forgot that I was wearing women's panties. I guess I'm so used to wearing them that I don't even think about it most of the time. I came to my senses and suddenly remembered that I was wearing panties, but it was too late—for a few of the onlookers were already giggling. I wasn't wearing a coat, and my polo shirt had no appreciable tail. When I went to cover my ass with my hands, I felt this big, gaping hole all the way up the back seam of my slacks!

As I was beating a hasty retreat out of an "employees only" door, I heard a little girl say to her mom, "Mommy, that man's wearing girl's underpants!" This comment was followed by titters and snickers from the other shoppers. I sprinted through the warehouse only to realize that my car was on the other side of the building.

I looked around. Nobody was in the warehouse. I grabbed—no, I *stole*—a beat-up shop coat that was hanging in the warehouse office. I made my way coolly back to my car. I called my wife on the car phone to tell her what had happened. She laughed hysterically and accused me of engineering the stunt on purpose to "show off my cute little panties."

When I got home, my wife had laid out a new pair of slacks for me on our bed. Next to them were a pair of her crotchless panties.

"What are these for?" I asked.

"Well, I figured that since you like to show off so much, the next time your slacks 'accidentally' rip, you can show off some skin! Maybe you'll even make some new and interesting friends that way!"

I'm so glad that my wife indulges me. Sometimes when the kids are at my mom's for the night, I'll throw all of my panties on the bed and me and my wife have at it. If you've never done it on a pile of 2,100 panties, you just don't know what you're missing! It's fun because you can literally cover yourself from head to toe in panties, just like you can with sand at the beach. It's a very sensual experience.

Is Bob normal? He has a degree in mechanical engineering. He works in manufacturing and made about $55,000 last year. He has three children who know nothing of his hobby. Bob is a family man who seems highly functional and satisfied. If you didn't know about his hobby, you'd never guess—unless, of course, you were in the carpet store that day!

Fetishists like Bob generally stay in the closet because it's simply too risky for a man to venture out in public wearing only a pair of flowered panties. Of course, there are cases reported every year of men being arrested for running about in public places wearing only a bra or some other item of women's clothing. The combination of fetishism and exhibitionism is not uncommon in the world of cross-dressing. What makes fetishism so interesting is the intriguing diversity and perverse enthusiasm displayed by the fetishistic. I mean, if a guy's running around in public dressed only in bra and panties, you just know that he must be having some kind of fun!

Fetishism rarely appears in women. Why? Some theorists have speculated that the absence of fetishism in women has to do with the fact that there are few, if any, taboos or social restrictions keeping women from wearing any item of men's clothing. But I think it's more than that. In particular, I think that women's clothing, especially their undergarments, have a greater inherent tactile and visual sensuality than do men's. Hence, there is more in women's clothing for a man to find erotic than vice versa. After all, what's to get excited about when it comes to a pair of boxer shorts?

In my mind, for example, a pair of white cotton BVDs cannot possibly compare in sensuality to a lacy pair of pink nylon bikini panties. Reading this, the alert therapist would say, "Aha! Would you rather have sex with the panties or the woman in the panties?" This question supposedly marks the dividing line between the fetishist and the "normal" man: The extreme fetishist would want only the panties; the mild fetishist would either want himself, or the woman, to wear the panties during sex; the "normal" man would want only the woman, and the panties would be incidental.

A SUBSPECIALTY WITHIN PANTY FETISHISM

Panty fetishists are not all like Bob. Some insist on obtaining used panties. Until recently the only way to procure soiled undies was to steal them. However, we live in an entrepreneurial age, and such theft is no longer necessary—thanks to what we could rightly call *niche marketing*. The following is a composite of certain ads typical of those seen in sexually oriented magazines:

> Pungent silk bikini panties worn by busty coeds during their sexy, sweaty, aerobic workouts. Panties $10.00 each (comes with two color photos). Specify size and color. Color choices: Black, pink, white, and lavender. Sixty-minute panty-workout video on VHS for $55.00 plus $3.50 shipping and handling. Call 1-800-xxx-xxxx to order or for our free catalogue of other sizzling hot fetish items and videos.

While certain of my readers are no doubt miffed that I omitted the 800 number, the rest of you are probably shaking your heads in disbelief. Is this really true? Are there really men who buy used panties, let alone sniff them? Well, Madonna knew what she was talking about when she asked David Letterman if he would like to sniff her panties. Mr. Letterman, somewhat aghast, declined Madonna's invitation. There were no doubt listeners in TV land who wished they were in the host's chair that night.

Judging by the proliferation of ads for used panties in sex publications, the used-lingerie market is a growth industry. And it's really no wonder that this business is growing when one considers that the used-panty business requires little or no start-up capital, no office or plant, no machinery or vehicles, and it is safe from product obsolescence and most product liability claims.

I'm sure a shrewd lawyer, however, could come up with an angle to sue a used-panty supplier. Imagine it: "Your honor, my client expected a pungent female musk as promised in the ad, and received only a slight aroma, a mere hint of a scent. There have been emotional damages and breach of contract. My client will settle for ten robustly pungent pairs and, well, throw in two pairs and a sweaty bra for me." Naturally, freshness dating would have to follow to guarantee consumer rights in the wake of this first trial.

It should be pointed out that panties are not the only game in town. Other popular fetish items are leather clothing, fur, high heels, garter belts and stockings, corsets, pantyhose, and rubber and vinyl clothing. These items can be employed alone or in combination, as in the case of the multiple fetishist.

FETISH THEFT

The male fetishist often goes to great lengths to secure the items of his desire. The man who takes a pair of panties that have been left in the dryer at a laundromat is not a thief. He is an opportunist who acts under the adage "Finders keepers, losers weepers." In this section, we're not discussing the opportunist, but rather those men who set out to purposely steal women's clothing. What motivates such men?

The embarrassment of buying women's panties or other items of clothing often, ironically, leads some fetishists to steal them. Other men, however, don't want new panties from Victoria's Secret; they want used undergarments that have been worn by women.

In July 1994, the Associated Press reported that a twenty-three-year-old man in Willoughby, Ohio, was arrested for breaking and entering. Upon searching his house and car, police found 450 assorted pieces of women's underwear. The culprit had stolen the underwear from laundry rooms at local apartment complexes during a two-year period.

The following month, the news services related the case of a man who was arrested for stealing panties from area clotheslines. In this case, the offender was caught redhanded by a hidden video camera as he plucked the panties from a line. Oddly enough, he had chosen the same time and day of the week to repeatedly raid the particular clothesline from which he was filmed stealing. The man was arrested and later led in front of the video cameras in handcuffs for the whole world to see.

Stories of "panty bandits" are not uncommon, yet they raise puzzling questions. If such men need panties so desperately, then why don't they simply visit Frederick's of Hollywood or buy used panties through the mail? With new and used panties so readily available in the marketplace, why do these men risk arrest and humiliating public exposure?

Underlying the excitement and risk of some theft is the unconscious need to be caught, exposed, humiliated, and punished. This need is typical of many who steal, not just the fetishist. Moreover, there is a difference between men such as Marla Maples's publicist—who steal a particular woman's clothing to establish an erotic connection with her—and men who steal from complete strangers. Aside from the need to get caught, then, the motives for fetish theft vary. Such acts can be viewed as aggression or as pathetic cries for help.

But the motive is not as important as the impact on the victim. It's illegal to steal. Further, when a hostile stranger invades one's privacy to steal things, rage and fear are natural responses. When that invasion and theft involves a woman's clothing, the woman may reasonably fear rape or murder as the next step.

For a man to put on, masturbate with, and ejaculate in a pair of stolen undies is viewed by many as a sort of quasi-rape that powerless men resort to when they've been unsuccessful in their relationships with women and their problems haven't been overcome with counseling. Fetish theft is immature and self-centered; it is a behavior that indicates a need for therapy or even incarceration.

Do all fetishists and CDs steal women's clothing? Certainly not. While it's impossible to quantify what percent of the CD population engages in this deplorable behavior, the overwhelming majority of CDs, in my experience, do not steal anything. But those who wish to vilify CDs have certainly used fetish theft as an excuse to do so. Consider the following mean-spirited characterization by Louise Kaplan in her 1991 book *Female Perversions:*

> A transvestite . . . can't get enough of touching women's clothing, buying it, stealing it. . . . He is obsessed with planning his next masturbatory ritual, deciding which clothes he will wear, and where, when, and if he should or should not steal them.

To believe Ms. Kaplan might well be to believe that each and every CD in the entire world is utterly consumed by the continual theft of women's clothing. Such reductionist thinking is remarkable only for its naïveté.

THE TRANSITIONAL FETISHIST

When the fetishist graduates to cross-dressing, the results can be fascinating to observe. The *transitional fetishist* (TF) is a term I've coined to describe the fetishist who is progressing out of strict, one-object fetishism and into complete cross-dressing.

This progression is provocative in psychological terms. I agree with the theory that fetishism begins when a young boy, for whatever reason, cannot possess the love and affection of his mother. Accordingly, he selects a symbolic substitute—say, an object of her clothing—to represent the affections of his mother. This happens in early childhood and is not a conscious act on the boy's part.

The object symbolizes a reality he cannot attain. It generates in him those positive feelings that result from maternal love and assurance that he cannot receive otherwise. There is clearly no inner feminine self operative in fetishism. Rather, there is an urge to symbolically possess the mother.

How does it happen that a fetishist graduates into complete cross-dressing? My theory is that when a fetishist comes to some resolution—usually through therapy—about his early relationship to his mother, the fetishistic impulse diffuses from the sharp focus of the mother into a more generalized emphasis upon the symbols of women. The shift in emphasis, however, corresponds to the template of fetishism in that a woman is still being sought.

Why does the fetishist evolve into a CD when he resolves his relationship to his mother? Why doesn't he simply abandon his fetishism and return to a more normative form of sexual expression? While this may happen in certain cases, I believe that the likelihood is that the fetishist, because he has been emotionally and orgasmically conditioned to associate pleasure with women's clothing, will not abandon this form of enjoyment.

Given that his sexuality has been molded from an early age by fetishism, it is reasonable to assume that the fetishistic impulse would be transformed into cross-dressing rather than returning to a "normative" condition, particularly since the fetishist has never known a normative condition.

When a fetishist begins to resolve the unconscious emotional issues that motivated his early sexuality, I have observed that he may begin to move away from fetishism. He starts by expressing his sexuality differently. Whereas his emotional perimeter had been represented by one or two items of female clothing, he now expands beyond that border by engaging in a more complete, though still fetishistic, form of cross-dressing.

It seems to me that the state of transitional fetishism is crucial—because it involves the re-cognition of fetishism. The most obvious way to re-cognize fetishism would be to postulate an inner feminine self and to thus begin to clothe that self. The CD's creation of a femme self represents an unconscious triumph over fetishism. There is no longer a lonely, guilty male masturbating in, for example, a pair of panties. Instead, the creation of the femme self allows the transitional fetishist to become the very image of that which he could only partially possess as a fetishist.

While there are CDs who claim to have never gone through the fetishistic stage, I've noticed that such CDs nevertheless exhibit transvestic obsession in the introductory phase of their cross-dressing. For this reason, I contend that cross-dressing cannot begin above the level of transitional fetishism—the exception being the peripheral CD.

Transitional fetishism is often characterized by an obsessive preoccupation with things feminine, particularly in seeing what one looks like when dressed as a woman. The emphasis on the artifacts of femininity, on contemplating one's femme self in the mirror, and frequent masturbation mark this state.

To call such behavior an expression of a femme self is somewhat ludicrous and self-serving. The use of the term *femme self* in this aspect of cross-dressing is no more than a charitable euphemism for obsession; it is a shared conceit of those who do not wish to trouble an otherwise grand and fascinating experience. The phase of transitional fetishism, incidentally, can last for a very long time because it is so pleasurable. The obsessed, after all, have good reasons for being that way!

At a PPOC meeting, I once saw a striking ensemble worn by a transitional fetishist whom I shall call Brenda. Brenda's outfit featured a leopard print vinyl mini, fishnet stockings with garter tabs showing, thigh-high black leather boots with five-inch heels, a gold lamé blouse strained beyond credibility by an overstuffed bra, and a platinum-blond wig. This was a stunning example of multiple fetishism if I've ever seen one.

My friend's wife, Rhonda, was visiting that same meeting. She remarked rather cattily to me that "real women don't dress like that."

Unable to resist the temptation to tease a real woman, I replied, "Well, Rhonda, maybe not here in the conservative Republican suburbs where you live, but I understand the look is *très chic* in Paris. Maybe you're just jealous that you can't dress like that."

"You queens disgust me," Rhonda sneered as she turned and strode away in her sensible shoes.

Breathtaking as this ensemble was, it revealed that cross-dressing, in the case of the TF, is no more than an aggregate whose sum total adds to the fetishistic interpretation of a woman. Rhonda had reacted angrily to the fact that a man could reduce a woman to a bizarre series of fetishes, particularly because she felt that those fetishes reflected the whorish fascinations of a warped male mind.

But what was truly going on in Brenda's head? Why would he dress like this? I liken him to a young girl who's just starting to use cosmetics and dress like a "big girl." A man tends to exaggerate when he first starts cross-dressing—just as a teenage girl might exaggerate when she starts experimenting with adult cosmetics and fashion.

The novice CD's fascinations and fetishes rise quickly to the surface. He wants to know what all of those things he has found so sexy are about. Why should he wear pantyhose when he can wear a garter belt and seamed stockings? What does it feel like to be busty? What usually emerges is his repressed adolescent fantasy of a "sexy" woman.

When I was growing up in the sixties, I used to read my mother's magazines. My fantasy woman was the mythical woman depicted in the Frederick's of Hollywood ads in the back of those magazines. Although she was only a drawing, she captivated my young mind as the embodiment of femininity: teased blond hair, heavy eyeliner, black lace panties and torpedo bra, diaphanous dresses, garter belt, stockings, and high heels.

I wanted to dress and look like the Frederick's woman, so when I first started cross-dressing, guess who I tried to look like? I wasn't trying to be a walking catalogue of fetishes, nor was I out to insult women. Rather, I wanted to emulate the Frederick's woman. I wanted to become her. I wanted to be a beautiful woman just like her. And I did, for I became like my idol by wearing the things that she wore.

FETISHISM DOWN UNDER

In this section, we will consider the case of Nigel. Nigel is an example of a man who moved from fetishism to cross-dressing. Nigel still retains his passion for his first love, satin slips, and, thanks to the moderating influence of his wife, doesn't display the excesses of other transitional fetishists.

Nigel is a six-foot-four-inch CD who lives in Melbourne, Australia. Sometimes when he is walking down the street *en femme* he might overhear one bloke say to another, "Now there's a bloody tall sheila!"—*sheila* being the Aussie term used to describe the CD. It's not necessarily a term of disrespect—cross-dressing is much more accepted in Australia than it is in the United States.

Nigel sometimes laughs when he hears himself called a sheila, because the origins of his fetishism, and in turn his cross-dressing, were so improbable. Who would think that a wool blanket would later turn into a fondness for slips? Nigel recalls the association that laid the foundation for his later cross-dressing:

It was the winter of 1958. I was eight years old and my great-uncle Bruce, to whom I was very close, had died while on business in Jakarta [Indonesia]. My parents had to fly there to bring him home. I was sent to stay at my aunt and uncle's house in Brisbane.

The first night there I was crying and very upset. My aunt Jayne bundled up with me in a wool blanket in front of the fireplace. She gave me a small drink of brandy and a cup of hot cocoa. She told me that Uncle Bruce had been sick for a very long time but now he was in heaven with God and the angels.

I remember that as she talked, I started almost hypnotically rubbing the satin liner on the blanket between my forefinger and thumb. It felt very reassuring, very comforting. I soon fell into a deep sleep. After that experience, I started to rub the satin liner on my own blankets before I fell asleep at night. It got to be a soothing habit that I didn't think about and no one ever noticed.

When I was fourteen, my parents decided to send me to a prep school in London. It was arranged that my mother should fly there with me for the interview. We planned to spend a fortnight in London so she could acquaint me with the town and introduce me to some old friends of hers who would act as my chaperons.

We arrived at Heathrow, had supper, and then checked into an elegant hotel in the West End. As I was becoming a young man now, my mother booked us into separate rooms. After supper, my mother retired to her room. I went to my room and began to unpack. As I was putting my things away into a chest of drawers I came upon a ladies' full slip. Apparently the former occupant of the room had failed to spot it while packing.

I pulled it out of the drawer and inspected it. It was a very fancy pale blue satin slip accented with delicate lace embroidery. I was familiar with the feel of satin, but this slip felt much more exquisite than anything I'd ever touched on a blanket. I became aroused in a way I'd not experienced hitherto. Feeling my reaction to be unseemly, I hid the slip in my suitcase. I was too embarrassed to ring the hotel operator and report that I'd found it, so I determined to discreetly dispose of the garment in a waste receptacle the next day.

I straightaway got into my pajamas and retired. As I lay in bed I began to rub the satin lining of the blanket. This caused me to begin to imagine how good the slip might feel on my body. I soon had a stiffy that wouldn't go away. I rationalized that there wouldn't be any harm in at least looking at the slip, so I retrieved it from my suitcase.

I lay in my bed and looked at the slip in the pale glow cast by the night-light; it felt wonderful and smelled of a faint jasmine perfume. I knew what I wanted to do next. Instead of thinking about it, because then I might talk myself out of it, I disrobed and slid the slip over my shoulders. As the cool satin snaked down my warm body it felt wonderful against my skin. I began to fondle myself through the slip and to think of the beautiful woman to whom it might have belonged.

A few minutes later and it was over; I had soiled the garment. I washed it in the bathroom sink and dried it with a towel the best I could. I then hung it on a floor lamp over the heat register. I laid awake most of the night with my mood alternating between shame and fascination.

In the morning my mother rang me up to make sure I was awake. She told me to meet her for breakfast in an hour. The slip was almost dry so I put it in my suitcase. I had no intention of repeating the shameful episode of the previous night, but my feelings soon overcame me and I found myself again stretched out on the bed, attired in this glorious garment.

I had just finished washing it again when my mother began knocking on my door. I quickly wrapped it in a bath towel and stuffed it into my suitcase. I spent the rest of the day in a fog, preoccupied with thoughts of what had happened and how good it had felt.

Even though it's now quite frayed and hasn't fit me in years, I still have that slip. It's like an old friend. My love for slips started in that hotel room, and it's never waned. I guess I have around fifty slips in my collection now; most of them, believe it or not, are gifts from my wife. The first time we made love, she undressed and had on a beautiful slip. I commented offhandedly about how beautiful it was, so she kept it on. I was in heaven making love to a woman who was wrapped in a lovely slip. She soon caught on to the true nature of my fancy, and she's indulged me ever since.

After we were married a bit, my wife encouraged me to dress like a woman for a summer costume party we attended while vacationing in London. I had so much fun getting dressed that I realized there was more to life than slips. Slowly my cross-dressing desires emerged, and my wife was always there to support me. In retrospect, it seems that I was destined to become a cross-dresser, for I have very strong feelings in that direction, yet I still wonder how my life might have turned out had I not found that slip in the hotel. I guess some later encounter with a slip would have triggered my desires.

At that fateful summer costume party in London, Nigel was indeed infected with the English disease—a British euphemism that refers to the preponderance of cross-dressing on the island nation. Cross-dressing in England and Australia is a familiar behavior that most people do not seem terribly bothered by, except in scandalous cases such as that of Stephen Milligan.

Milligan, a noted member of Parliament, was found dead in his apartment in 1992. He was bound and gagged, had a plastic bag over his head, and was wearing only a garter belt and stockings. Stories also abound that certain of the Queen's male servants are themselves queens—but I digress.

Nigel claims that the basis of his fetishism and cross-dressing is rooted in the satin liner of a blanket. In Nigel's case, a soothing tactile experience later cascaded into a sexual preference for slips in particular and women's clothing in general. But this is not all that unusual, for as Nigel's wife says, "A proper lady should always wear a slip under her dress!"

WHAT IS FETISHISM?

What motivates Bob or Nigel? Why are they so turned on by women's underwear? The usual response is to say that men have fetishes. But what is a fetish, and why do only men seem to have them?

The basic boundary between male and female is marked by clothing—or is it? These days females can wear any article of male clothing without censure, including boxer shorts. But let a man put on a pink skirt and he's branded a cross-dresser. Worse, let him put on a pair of pink panties and he's branded a fetishist.

The clothing boundary between male and female seems to be a one-way border these days: Females can cross into the realm of male clothing freely, whereas men are still widely vilified as perverts for crossing the border into the land of female clothing. Is this not hypocritical?

Some feminist educators have advocated that women use vibrators to achieve sexual gratification. Does this practice make a woman sexually fetishistic? A fetishist has been classically defined as a person who derives sexual gratification from a nonsexual part of the body or an inanimate object. Yet a woman who masturbates with a vibrator is not considered fetishistic. If anything, this practice is viewed as a sensuous form of autoeroticism in which the vibrator is but a benign mechanism of pleasure.

But let a man masturbate with a woman's high-heeled shoe and he is condemned as fetishistic. What's the difference between these two cases? Both a vibrator and a shoe are objects that can be used to achieve sexual gratification. A supposed difference is that the vibrator has been specifically designed for sexual purposes, whereas the shoe is a nonsexual object that has been imbued with erotic qualities by the fetishist.

The apparent logic is that the masturbatory use of a "sexual device" is not fetishistic, while the masturbatory use of a nonsexual object is. It seems that it is the attribution of erotic qualities to a nonsexual object, and the subsequent act of masturbation with that object, that constitutes the charge of fetishism. This dilemma having been solved, we can now say with certainty that a man who has intercourse with an inflatable love doll is not abnormal because a love doll is a sexual device.

"Now you just hold your horses, Mister Smarty-Pants," the person-on-the-street might insist. "A man who has intercourse with a love doll is pathetic." Perhaps the love-doll-lover is pathetic. But if he is, then isn't the woman who uses a vibrator also pathetic?

Most people would probably say she is not, for it seems that there is a decided bias in favor of women when it comes to what is essentially a matter of sexual aesthetics: The image of a woman pleasuring herself with a vibrator is more attractive than that of a man masturbating into a shoe or humping an inflatable love doll in a cheap hotel room!

It is evident that sexual fetishism, like penis envy, is a concept flawed by both a clinical and cultural bias. In the case of penis envy, it's easier to accept that a girl can be envious that she doesn't have a penis than it is to accept that a boy can suffer vagina envy. Nevertheless, certain analysts, most notably psychologist Bruno Bettleheim in 1954, have reported cases of what could be called breast and vagina envy in boys.

Still, it seems culturally absurd for a man, the proud owner of a status-giving penis, to be envious of the vagina, that Freudian void into which he could fall and be devoured. Most men would heatedly deny an envy of the vagina for the same reason that women might deny that they can be fetishistic: Culture has certain sexual biases that we tend to embrace.

I think that much of what it called fetishism reflects the taboo against the full expression of male sensuality. In the next section, we will explore the subject of fetishism in an attempt to reveal the prejudices upon which it is built.

MALES AND FETISHISM: GUILTY UNTIL PROVEN INNOCENT

A person who has unusual tastes in food is different from a bulimic; an exotic preference for foods is not the same as an eating disorder. And so it follows that a male who demonstrates an interest in women's clothing is not necessarily fetishistic. Yet a man who displays such an interest comes under much more severe scrutiny than the gourmet who orders a jellied squid burrito.

Consider the example of a young boy who has a pleasurable tactile and visual response to a piece of his mother's clothing, say a lacy, red silk camisole. What is happening in this case? The boy touches silk and finds that he enjoys its smooth, luxurious feel. He sees the color red and the intricate lace and considers it to be pretty. In and of itself, this could be considered an aesthetic and tactile experience rather than a fetishistic one. But what happens when he wants to again enjoy the experience that the camisole gave him? Is this where the young boy crosses the line into fetishism?

Culturally, a boy is not supposed to have such desires in the first place. While a single experience can be dismissed as curiosity, a boy's repeated interest in his mother's clothing is a cause for concern to his parents because boys are expected to show little or no interest in women's clothing.

The parents' question can become one of motive: Is a boy's interest in his mother's clothing merely an aesthetic and tactile experience, or is it a precursor of adult fetishism or transvestism? Further, with what is the child associating his mother's clothing? Love he does not receive? Nascent sexuality? The question may assume even greater importance if the parents see their young son develop an erection in the presence of his mother's clothing. Will such an experience take root in the boy's unconscious, only to later bloom in puberty?

Also, what triggered the boy's interest in his mother's clothing? Was it simply sight and touch? A born predisposition? Did his mother unintentionally provide arousing cues? Is the boy escaping from the pressures of masculinity being exerted upon him?

There is certainly much scrutiny applied when a boy shows an interest in women's clothing. But let's reverse the situation. Let's say that the boy's mother wants to dress up her young daughter in the style of little Shirley Temple. She dresses the girl in a taffeta dress, crinolines, frilly panties, and patent leather shoes. The young girl is free to luxuriate in this clothing. Indeed, she's even encouraged to do so by her mother, grandmother, and aunts. "Oooh, you're so pretty," they coo. "Don't you just feel wonderful in those clothes?"

But then the unexpected happens. The young girl doesn't like the clothing. It feels itchy, tight, and constricting. She would rather wear jeans, a T-shirt, and cowboy boots because they feel more comfortable. Discouraged, her mother dismisses her as a "tomboy." She hopes that her daughter will grow out of this phase and come to accept the world of delicate clothing, lace, and cosmetics which culture has prepared for women.

Tomboyish behavior in girls isn't typically treated with the same concern as the behavior of boys who express an interest in women's clothing. If a young girl puts on her father's coat and tie it's cute; if a young boy puts on his mother's dress and heels it's a serious problem. The girl is merely idolizing her father; the boy is suspected of showing signs of potential fetishism or transvestism.

What has happened in both cases is that the child has had a tactile and visual experience of clothing. He or she has indicated a preference for certain fabrics and clothing. But since we use clothing to symbolically separate the sexes, a problem has been created for the young boy.

The nature of this problem is twofold. First, it is culturally frowned upon, at least in terms of clothing, for boys to express an enjoyment of the *full range* of sight, touch, color, fabric, and clothing. Conversely, girls are encouraged to enjoy the *full range* of sight, touch, color, fabric, and clothing. Girls can enjoy cotton blue jeans, pink nylon dresses, lavender silk jackets, and so forth; boys, lest they be considered effeminate, must limit their apparel to specific fabrics, colors, and clothing. True, fashion choices have broadened for males, but there still exists a decided line a male shouldn't cross.

Second, if a boy walks into the living room dressed in his mother's pearls, dress, and heels he may incur the harsh judgment of family and culture. Conversely females can play with the symbols of masculinity without penalty.

The bias clearly favors females, for the girl is cute while the boy's behavior is often condemned. Yet is the boy truly showing fetishistic or transvestic behavior? Or is he simply ignorant of culture's sense of symbolic propriety? Indeed, is it possible that he is merely enjoying the sight and touch of those symbols of the opposite sex which he considers to be beautiful?

In this hypothetical example, it is possible that the boy could be showing nothing more than a passing interest in women's clothing. Yet parents and culture react with alarm because they don't like such displays of curiosity: Males are guilty of fetishism until proven innocent! How did culture get to the point where a man's sensuality is so suspect?

THE HISTORY OF FETISHISM

The word *fetish* is derived from the Portuguese *feitiço*, which refers to a charm or the act of sorcery. This word was introduced into the West by eighteenth-century European travelers and anthropologists, who first used it to characterize the religious objects used by the tribesmen of the Guinea coast and believed by them either to be inhabited by a spirit or to possess magical powers.

In this day and age, fetishes are not well understood. In a sense, a fetish could be thought of as a celebrity's possession. We somehow feel connected to a celebrity if we have her autograph or something that belongs to her. Likewise, a person may feel connected to a spiritual entity by virtue of a fetish because the fetish is believed to be imbued with the mystical power of a given spiritual being. Amulets, charms, and talismans are types of fetishes.

To the eighteenth-century mind, *fetishism* (the practice of using fetishes) carried with it the implication that a fetish was a mere object to which an ignorant person, or a "savage," had attributed spiritual powers. This conception, arising within the context of the Age of Enlightenment, made sense at the time. With its emphasis on reason and intellect, the Enlightenment sought to destroy superstition, and particularly religious superstition.

Enlightenment thinkers were not known to treat religion gently, or to respect non-European cultures. Dinesh D'Souza, in his controversial book *The End of Racism,* argues that racism is a product of the Enlightenment. This is hardly a revelation, for the notion that the nonwhite races were inferior was widely accepted within an eighteenth-century Europe heady with the prospects of world domination.

That the flawed concepts of fetishism and racism are rooted in an eighteenth-century bias against religion and non-European races is not surprising. What is surprising is how staunchly many racial and psychological bigots still defend these concepts. It is more fascinating yet to realize that the stigma of fetishism has always been there in the shadows to reinforce the claims of racism. After all, if one is going to denigrate an entire class of people, it is necessary to also invalidate their religious practices.

In particular, Christendom added its weight to the stigma of fetishism when its nineteenth-century missionaries propagated Christianity along with European culture and biases. Besides forcibly clothing the indigenous peoples—the so-called heathen—who preferred to live seminude in arid climes, Christendom perpetuated the definition of fetishism by applying the term to those religious practices and sacred objects it encountered in Africa, India, and other parts of the world.

Christendom characterized those who used fetishes as evil, ignorant, or both. The shaman was not respected as a holy man who used sacred images during the worship of his God. Instead, the shaman was denounced as a "witch doctor" and alternately portrayed as a backward savage who waved a dumb, wooden doll into an empty sky, or, worse, as a demoniac who was communing with the devil while in a hypnotic trance.

Stories abounded throughout nineteenth-century Christendom, and continue to this day, of missionaries bringing home fetishes to display in their homes, only to later discover, through a series of mysterious troubles visited upon them, that the objects were possessed by devils. Such stories were often spread to support the Christian bias that the devil inhabited fetishes and that they were a doorway for evil to enter one's home. In our day, for example, Ouija boards are still thought by some to be a fetish possessed of malevolent spirits.

Missionary tales also circulated which claimed that when a savage realized that it was he, and not his false god, who had imbued his fetish with power, the spell was broken. In this vein, fetishism took on the connotation of an ignorant practice that could be overcome by truth.

In using the term *fetish* to demean both non-European and non-Christian religious artifacts, it can be argued that Enlightenment thinkers and Christian missionaries employed the same tactic used by many groups today to defame their opponents. In the arena of political correctness, one risks being branded either racist or sexist for saying or doing anything that minorities or feminists do not like. In yesterday's arena of Protestant correctness, one could be labeled fetishistic if he used sacred objects in his worship of a non-Christian God. Christendom had a vested interest in perpetuating this intellectual conceit of the Enlightenment, for it served to make other religions seem crude and backward.

Christendom denounced kachina dolls, amulets, and the like while insisting that it was fetish-free. Yet, in the case of Christianity, God is believed to administer his will partly through the agency of his angels. Angels could thus be said to act conceptually as fetishes within Christendom. Whereas a non-Christian religion might locate an agent of the divine within an object, Christianity locates its divine agents within the angels.

So while the African tribesman might believe that the wooden hawk hung around his neck embodies a spirit that will protect him during his travels, the Christian believes that there is an invisible host of angels surrounding and protecting him lest he dash his foot upon a stone. The belief is the same; the only difference is that one fetish is visible while the other is not.

If angels approximate fetishes, the Catholic usage of the saints mirrors them, particularly with respect to the prayers and offerings that are made to the statues of the saints. During the Crusades the relics of the saints, or a "piece of the true cross," were venerated as sacred objects in the same way that fetishes are in other religions.

In the religious sense of the term, fetishism is nothing more than the use of sacred objects believed to possess spiritual power. If you examine any religion it is possible to find practices, symbols, or beliefs that qualify as fetishistic. *Fetishism* became a derogatory term because eighteenth-century intellectuals didn't care for religion and because nineteenth-century Christian missionaries wanted to utterly destroy competing religions. Both groups used the word *fetish* to propagate intolerance rather than enlightenment.

Late-nineteenth-century sexual theorists appropriated the concept of religious fetishism to describe the condition in which a person achieves sexual gratification from an inanimate object or a nonsexual body part rather than from another person. This "learned borrowing" was based upon the notion that in the same way a "savage" might attribute mystical powers to a mere object, so, too, might a neurotic attribute sexual qualities to an object or a nonsexual body part.

While Freud wasn't the first to make the comparison, the likening of religious fetishism to this particular sexual behavior is, in my mind, unfortunate, because the analogy carries with it an implicit stigma. In the same way that the "savage" with his fetish was deemed crude by the European intellectual, so, too, did the sexual fetishist come to be viewed as sexually crude.

DEFINING SEXUAL FETISHISM

How do we distinguish between legitimate sensuality and true sexual fetishism? Let's look at how Freud defined the issue. In order to clarify the following quote, I need to mention that while we normally refer to material things as *objects*, Freud said, "Let us call the person from whom sexual attraction proceeds the *sexual object* and the act towards which the instinct tends the *sexual aim.*" What Freud meant is that the *sexual object* is the person that one desires and the *sexual aim* is what one wants to do with that person. Thus, in his classic work *Three Essays on the Theory of Sexuality*, Freud defined sexual fetishism by stating:

> What is substituted for the sexual object is some part of the body (such as the foot or the hair) which is in general very inappropriate for sexual purposes, or some inanimate object which bears an assignable relation to the person whom it replaces and preferably to that person's sexuality (e.g., a piece of clothing or underlinen). Such substitutes are with some justice likened to the fetishes in which savages believe that their gods are embodied.

Freud developed his thinking further by stating:

> "A certain degree of fetishism is thus habitually present in normal love, especially in those stages of it in which the normal sexual aim seems unattainable or its fulfillment prevented . . . The situation becomes pathological when the longing for the fetish . . . actually *takes the place of* the normal aim . . . and becomes the sole sexual object [italics in the original].

According to Freud, pathological fetishism occurs when an object takes the place of the normal sexual aim. A fetish is classically considered to be a substitute. For example, we can take the case of a boy whose mother withholds love. Since his mother does not love him, the boy looks for some intimate symbol of her to possess: Panties, a perfumed nightgown, or shoes are typical.

Adoring and embracing an intimate object of his mother's becomes a coping strategy by which the boy can generate a sense of his mother's missing love. What caring person would not feel sympathy for such a child and hostility toward his mother? The child is committing no wrong; he is simply trying to fulfill his innate need for love.

Sexual fetishism, however, does not always begin with the search for a mother substitute. Fetishistic conditioning can occur, for instance, when a boy's psyche is somehow *imprinted* during a particularly critical or defining moment in his sexual development. The boy's nascent sexuality is said to be suddenly fixated by some powerful sexual stimulant.

Such sexual associations are typically unintended and made during childhood. The clinical literature is replete with case histories of men who have had powerful formative experiences in childhood that conditioned their later sexual preferences. Many of these experiences involved the accidental viewing of a partially clothed mother or other female relative, or being in a situation in which the smell or feel of an object gave them an overwhelming sense of comfort and security.

Childhood fetishism becomes sexual when a boy begins to masturbate with the object of his affection. When this happens, an indelible sexual association is made. This sexual association is said to be pathological if masturbation with the object becomes the young man's sole sexual outlet.

In contemporary clinical thought, fetishism is classed as a *paraphilia,* a condition in which sexual arousal and orgasm is achieved only by means of compulsive, or obligatory, dependence upon a personally or socially unacceptable stimulus. Fetishism, infantilism, transvestism, sadism, exhibitionism, and frotteurism are among the more than forty recognized paraphilias.

The problem with the notion of a paraphilia is twofold. First, who determines what is a socially unacceptable sexual stimulus? Obviously, those in the mental health field make the determination based on sexual norms. Heterosexual intercourse could be said to be a compulsive sexual stimulus, yet it is deemed socially acceptable and thus normal. The bell curve of the heterosexual majority prevails in the matter of defining acceptable sexual behavior. This approach ignores the continuum of human sexuality and instead creates a tacit sexual caste system in which heterosexuals reign and all others are unclean.

Second, if a sexual stimulus such as lingerie is enjoyed by a man but he does not habitually require it for arousal and orgasm, is he still paraphilic? Is being "partly paraphilic" like being partly pregnant? Clinical assessments can sometimes fail to make such fine distinctions.

Are Bob and Nigel paraphilic? Both like to occasionally masturbate with women's underwear. They also report that women's underwear is sometimes involved when they make love. Nigel reports that slips are involved in his marital sex about one-quarter of the time, and that slip-wearing is usually initiated by his "rather randy" wife. Bob reports that panties are involved in less than 10 percent of his marital relations.

Bob and Nigel's fetishism—if that is indeed the right term for their behavior—is benign, for neither depends solely upon lingerie for sexual arousal or orgasm. They have both successfully integrated the sensual enjoyment of lingerie into their lives with the approval of their respective spouses. Their behavior, in my mind, does not merit the stigma of being called either paraphilic or fetishistic. In recognizing that male sensuality can extend to an appreciation of feminine clothing without necessarily being pathological, we can begin to distinguish fetishism from sensuality.

We can also recognize that there does indeed occur a condition whereby an individual's sexual expression is compulsively dependent upon a socially unacceptable sexual stimulus. If we were just discovering such behavior, it might be called EOOS (erotic object overvaluation syndrome), SOCD (sexual object choice disorder), or some other more clinically descriptive and humane term than *fetishism.* I favor the latter term—sexual object choice disorder—because it conveys a clinical description without impugning male sensuality or evoking religious imagery, as does the diagnosis of fetishism.

A key problem with the Freudian conception of fetishism is its determination that the association of sensuality and eroticism with anything but the "normal" sexual object, i.e. another person, is abnormal. Freud's presumption is that "inanimate objects" are inert and meaningless. But is lingerie no more than meaningless articles of clothing? Does the fetishist alone imbue lingerie with sexual meaning?

Of course not. Lingerie signifies the most intimate of female anatomy; it's hardly a neutral, meaningless object. Moreover, certain kinds of lingerie, such as black lace panties, are erotic by virtue of culture's attribution of eroticism to them. In the case of lingerie, then, the fetishist is not imbuing it with erotic qualities so much as he is responding, albeit "abnormally," to the prior erotic attribution made by his culture.

The definition of sexual fetishism also features the rather odd premise that there are sexual and nonsexual parts of the body. This arbitrary division limits sexuality to those high-traffic erotic areas of the body such as genitals, lips, and breasts. Yet who has not been so infatuated with another that everything about him seems wonderful, captivating, and sexual? Everything about a person with whom one is madly in love seems special and sexual—or at least potentially sexual if one is creative.

When making love it is not unusual to be so overcome with passion that one covers his lover with kisses from head to toe. Kissing the naked skin of another is sensual. Having a sexual enthusiasm for a particular part of the human anatomy is also sensual and quite normal. Buttocks, thighs, hips, stomachs, pectorals, shoulders, necks, and hair are common "nonsexual" areas of the body people enjoy kissing and caressing during lovemaking.

Men and women who wish to further enjoy their erotic enthusiasms can always go to a bar and watch exotic dancers strip. Men who enjoy seeing women's breasts can view them anytime of the day or night at many clubs throughout the world. Likewise, women who lust after the male chest can enjoy the writhing, naked male chests at similar establishments. An attraction for the feet, however, is considered fetishistic.

Yet what's the difference between a sexual attraction for one body part versus another? While the foot as an object of sexual excitement seems unusual, there is nothing inherently repulsive about the foot or about someone who wants to kiss the foot of another. If a man wants to ejaculate onto a woman's feet, he is said to be fetishistic. However, if another man wants to ejaculate onto his wife's breasts, thus giving her the manly "pearl necklace," he is considered to be neither fetishistic nor neurotic. That the classical definition of fetishism would impose such limits on eroticism betrays its nineteenth-century Victorian inhibition.

What becomes clear when one attempts to clarify fetishism is that male sensuality and sexuality are both easily stigmatized. The CD suffers in particular because culture balances male sexuality precariously upon a Beach Boys motif of heterosexual athleticism that leaves little room for those who prefer stockings to surfboards. Thus, the CD wipes out in the big waves of culture because he has bad psychoanalytic karma. You dig?

4

COSMETIC CROSS-DRESSERS

The presence of an inner feminine self, and the need to express that self, is what differentiates the cosmetic CD from the fetishist. The cosmetic CD dresses fully as a woman, including wearing cosmetics and wig, to give life to the feminine nature he feels inside.

The first step the cosmetic CD takes in bringing his feminine self to life is to give her a name. The second step is to bring her out of the closet and into the light of day. This difficult step involves telling others that he is a CD.

Confession is a watershed in the world of cross-dressing, for it signifies that a man has finally begun to come to terms with the fact that he is a CD. For a few cosmetic CDs, the final step is in allowing the feminine self to participate in a sexual relationship with a man. This is more difficult yet, for there are issues of bisexuality or homosexuality that must be considered along with those of cross-dressing.

In this chapter we'll meet the three subtypes of the cosmetic CD: the closet CD, the social CD, and the she-male. These subtypes essentially represent lifestyle choices. There is no evidence to suggest that a closet CD, for example, will turn into a she-male.

The notion of the feminine self, or the "femme self" as it is called in CD circles, will also be discussed. The femme self is the paradox of cross-dressing. It is tremendously liberating for a CD to acknowledge his feminine self, yet that same feminine self can become a demon in whom hides the worst aspects of the male CD's personality. As with any suspicious character, we will keep the femme self under close surveillance as we continue on our journey.

WHEN DOES ONE BECOME A CROSS-DRESSER?

A woman I dated once asked me, "When did you decide to become a cross-dresser?" It was an interesting question. In my case, I started out playing with my sister's underwear and gradually experimented with other items. I didn't become a true CD until I was twenty-six.

Statistically, Dr. Docter tells us that the majority of CDs first cross-dress between the ages of five and ten and make their first cross-dressed public appearance between the ages of twenty-one and thirty. In terms of sexual orientation, Docter reports that fully 97 percent of the CDs surveyed in his book described themselves as "exclusively or predominantly heterosexual."

It takes tremendous courage for a man to come to terms with being a cross-dresser. He is usually motivated by a seemingly uncontrollable and incomprehensible sexual and emotional drive to cross-dress. This drive cannot be controlled by his own willpower or rationality, by therapy, or by threats from his girlfriend, wife, or parents.

Like a violent thunderstorm that sweeps across the desert, the urge to cross-dress has an engulfing, irrational power and urgency that cannot be ignored or denied. Cross-dressing comes upon a man as both a crisis and a relief. It is a crisis in that a man's sense of masculinity, respectability, and propriety is challenged; it is a relief in that a man can finally surrender to his desire to immerse himself in femininity.

The decision to "become a cross-dresser" is a difficult one, but the decision having been made, the CD must get on with his life. The question is no longer "Am I a cross-dresser?" but rather "What do I do now?" The emphasis for most CDs is not on staying in the closet, but on somehow trying to tell a wife or a girlfriend about their secret life. My friend Lincoln (Sherri) has something to say about this:

> I struggled with the question of whether or not I was a cross-dresser for almost ten years. I tried to talk to my wife about it, but she threatened to divorce me if I ever became "one of those." The

urges were just too great, however, and I found that I was spending my time sneaking around to dress up and worried that my wife would find the things I had hidden.

When I finally admitted to myself and my wife that I was a CD, she hit the roof. "I would never have married you if I knew this, you sonofabitch!" she yelled. "How could you do this to me? What am I going to find out next, that you're gay?"

I asked my wife if she would get into therapy with me, but she refused. She filed for divorce shortly thereafter. She said that she "wanted to be married to a man, not a woman." It broke my heart. I gave up cross-dressing for a year after that, but the desires wouldn't go away. For me, cross-dressing isn't enough to build my whole life around, but on the other hand it's an undeniable part of who I am. What am I going to do?

Cross-dressing can carry an enormous price tag, particularly if the CD announces his status after he's been married or if his wife accidentally discovers him—as did the fictional John's wife in the beginning of the book. In the absence of a supportive wife, Lincoln did the next best thing: He reached out to find those who could offer him empathy and fellowship.

I think that a man truly becomes a CD when he announces it to himself and others, particularly his wife and fellow CDs. Short of this declaration, there is only a lonely man who is struggling with his secret desire to dress like a woman. A true CD is someone who can admit to himself and those close to him that he enjoys and participates in this activity. Such acknowledgment is the difference between the pain of secrecy and the freedom of truth.

THE CLOSET AND COMING OUT OF IT

When I speak of my having "come out of the closet," I am making something of a misstatement, for I let only certain friends, coworkers, and family members know that I was a CD. I did not announce it to the public at large, nor do I volunteer the information when I meet complete strangers. I did come out of a literal closet though, joined a CD club, and became semipublic about my cross-dressing.

The decision to come out of the closet must be made with great care. In my case, my wife has definite objections to my coming fully out of the closet because she feels it would hurt our two children. I agree. I would never want my kids to be the butt of cruel jokes at school, nor would I look forward to the problems it could create for me at work. It is out of this same concern for the well-being of my family that I used a pen name to write this book.

While some activists might well pronounce me a coward, I feel that my staying semipublic is what any caring parent would do for the good of his children. After all, discretion is the better part of valor. I recommend that the closeted CD begin by sharing his secret only with those close to him or in a support group of other CDs.

The next two stories contrast life inside and outside of the closet. The contrast will illustrate the tension that a CD must live with when he keeps his deepest secret hidden.

A CLOSET CROSS-DRESSING POLICEMAN

Randy is forty years old and a fourteen-year veteran police officer. He formerly worked narcotics as an undercover officer and is currently a patrol sergeant. Randy is a six-foot-two-inch, 210-pound man who carries a 9mm Browning semiautomatic pistol strapped to his side. He doesn't take flak from people and is as conservative a voter as you'd care to meet. Randy likes to occasionally dress as a woman in his off hours when his wife and children are away. He does so about twice a month.

Randy is what you might call a closet queen, only you would never call him that to his face. A more charitable description would be to call him a closet cross-dresser. Randy's wife didn't find out about his interest until several years after they were married. He was afraid to let her know because she had always told him that she loved his masculinity and that she had married a cop to feel protected.

Randy's biggest problem with his cross-dressing is his loneliness. Concerned about protecting his job, he discussed this topic with only two people until he was almost forty: a therapist and myself. The therapist, a friend of mine, urged Randy to speak to me so that he could at least see that there were other men like him.

I first met Randy in 1988 for lunch at an out-of-the-way location. Initially we were awkward and uncomfortable, but we broke the ice talking about the manly subjects of handguns and fighter aircraft. We didn't get around to the topic of cross-dressing until after we left the restaurant and went to a local airport to watch planes land. There, in the privacy of the outdoors, Randy opened up to me as a friend.

Randy maintained that he would remain in the closet at least as long as he was on the force, and probably for the rest of his life. He said he was too inhibited to explore his cross-dressing fully and refused to join a CD club. When I told him I thought that most of what he does when he's dressed amounts to no more than guilty masturbation, he agreed. Yet he was not prepared to do anything about his current state of affairs.

"I'd shoot myself before I'd ever let myself become a full-blown cross-dresser. It would just be too big of a shock to my wife and kids. I'm the husband, I'm the dad, I'm the cop— How could I ever let myself become something that would ruin my life? But sometimes the urge to dress up like a woman is so goddamn intense. Especially after I've had a hard day at work."

Soon after our meeting, Randy called me when he was home alone. He was drunk. He told me that he liked me a lot, but that he sort of thought of me as his "transvestite friend" that he was ashamed to have. I told him that the real transvestite he was ashamed of was himself. He grew silent and then apologized. Randy never gave me his phone number, and it was a long time before we spoke again. When he did call me back, he admitted that he had a problem with alcohol.

"My job is so stressful," he lamented, "that the only way I can unwind is to get drunk. And when I get drunk, I like to dress up because that's the only way I let myself enjoy it. It's a goddamn vicious cycle, and it's killing me."

For the man who has not accepted his cross-dressing, nothing is worse than compounding it with chemical dependency and guilt. This hellish combination requires professional intervention. Even without the problem of substance abuse, the closet can be a dark and lonely place. My advice for any closeted CD is to at least make contact with a support group in your area. There is a list of such clubs in Appendix A of this book. Interaction and socialization are powerful tools for getting out of the closet and feeling more normal about yourself.

Randy's therapist eventually convinced him to join an out-of-town CD club under an assumed name. Because he could go to the meeting early and get dressed in one of the hotel rooms set aside for this purpose, few in the club ever saw what he looked like as a man. After a year of meeting other people and making a few friends, Randy finally realized that he wasn't a monstrous pervert. Only then was he able to confront his alcoholism and admit himself to an in-patient treatment facility.

The last time I saw Randy, his therapy had progressed to the point where he had told his wife. She was not, he reported, very happy, but she was willing to work on her issues with it in therapy because, as she said, she loved Randy very much. I knew that he was no longer fighting a war with himself when he told me that he had chosen the name Jennifer for his femme self.

THE SOCIAL CROSS-DRESSER

Just as marijuana may lead to heroin, wearing panties may lead to wearing bras, garter belts, stockings, high heels, dresses, wigs, and cosmetics. A fairly typical pattern that has been identified among CDs is for the behavior to begin in childhood when a young boy plays with some article of his mother's clothing. This behavior then normally diminishes and resurfaces at puberty. Many young boys go through a phase in which they play with their mother's clothing and cosmetics, and it has no lasting effects. For the future CD, however, such play makes a powerful and lasting impression.

A question that therapists are occasionally asked by concerned parents is: "Our son is playing with his mother's clothes. Is he going to grow up to be a transvestite?" From my point of view, this is an age-dependent question. In most cases, such childhood cross-dressing is experimental and does not ensure adult cross-dressing. However, if an adolescent boy is masturbating with women's clothing, particularly lingerie, then he will more than likely mature into a fetishist or a CD.

Unlike childhood play, once the intensity and pleasure of orgasm becomes associated with women's clothing, a powerful psychosexual conditioning process has taken place. It is unlikely that such conditioning can be reversed. We inherently seek pleasure and avoid pain. And to the extent that fetish masturbation is a pleasurable escape from an adolescent's pain, it becomes all the more reinforced.

In handling childhood cross-dressing it is critically important not to invalidate the child. Criticizing a boy's cross-dressing will only make him become clandestine about the behavior. The secrecy only reinforces the guilt and drives a wedge between parent and child. Children should always be made to feel that they can ask their parents for help with anything. If a child feels his parents will judge or punish him for his behavior, he will not ask for their help. Acceptance and understanding is the first step in helping a child to deal with a behavior he cannot fully comprehend himself.

Cross-dressing may stay at a fetish level for many years, involving nothing more than simple masturbation. As I've indicated, however, a fetish often triggers an underlying need to experience femininity, to find out what it would be like to look and feel like a woman. The decision to completely cross-dress, let alone come out of the closet, is an experience full of anxiety, for the line that is being crossed is a cultural and personal barrier about what it is to be a man.

Perhaps so many CDs stay in the closet because they fear that a public admission of cross-dressing is tantamount to an admission that they have failed as men. Certainly the first time a man dresses completely as a woman he may feel that he has surrendered his manhood to a monstrous passion. Let's have Gilbert tell us about the first time he dressed completely as a woman and how he came out of his closet:

> I've been a CD for about five years now. I use to be into just wearing pantyhose and high heels. I started wearing them in junior high

school and they remained all the "cross-dressing"—if you want to call it that—that I did until I was twenty-eight. It was then I began noticing how the women at my office dressed and looked. Their clothes and their look really turned me on. I found that I was even becoming jealous that women were allowed to wear such beautiful clothing and men couldn't.

I wanted to dress completely like a woman, but something inside wouldn't let me. I was torn between this intense desire to experience dressing like a woman and wanting to protect my manhood. Then one day a woman salesperson visited me to demonstrate some new emulator software. She looked so feminine, so sexy, so erotic, that I just said to myself, Damn it, I want to know what it feels like to dress like her. It was then that I decided to quit thinking about it and do it.

I was living by myself in West Los Angeles, so it wasn't like I had an issue with a girlfriend or a wife about wanting to dress up. My only problem was that I didn't know the first thing about how to dress like a woman. I didn't know anything about cosmetics, dress sizes, bra sizes, or wigs, or anything.

Thinking logically through the subject (I'm a software engineer), I first rented a "how-to" cosmetics video that Christie Brinkley had made to study cosmetics selection and application. Then I looked through a couple of women's fashion magazines to get ideas for what would look good on a six-foot, 175-pound woman.

I decided to buy my first set of clothes through mail order because I was just too embarrassed to go into a store. I went to Penneys and bought their catalogue. While looking through the "big girls" section, I found a size chart and figured out what sizes I would need. I went up to the next size just to be safe. I ordered a pretty nice pink sweater dress, a wide pink belt, a white lace bra, a three-pack of lace-trimmed bikini panties, and a white full slip; I already had all the pantyhose and high heels I would ever need. Rather than using my first name, I used my first initial on the order form and dropped it off at the local Penneys with my credit card number on it. I then took my cosmetics list and went to about six different stores to fill it so I wouldn't look suspicious buying all this makeup stuff at one store.

While waiting for my mail-order clothes, I practiced putting on my cosmetics like I'd seen in the video. I began by putting on my hose and heels; then I sat down in front of the bathroom mirror. I put on the base, powder, blush, eyeliner, and lipstick. By the time I got done I had such an erection from looking at myself in the mirror that I ejaculated without touching myself. It wasn't that I looked so hot, it was just that I had this wonderful, sexy feeling that I'd never had. I was hooked.

My clothes came in about a week. As soon as they arrived, I realized that I didn't have a wig. I really wanted one because I wanted to look as much like a woman as I could the first time I dressed up. I took the next afternoon off and drove over to Hollywood. Hollywood is so full of freaks that I didn't think anybody would notice if I bought a wig. I found a wig store on Hollywood Boulevard and went inside. There was an Asian lady working. I told her I wanted a wig for a costume party. She smiled knowingly and told me I was welcome to try on anything I wanted. I finally found a nice blond wig and paid her $108.45 for it. She did a quick comb out on it and attached it to a wig head and then placed it inside a brown plastic bag. I headed back home for my big night.

I was so turned on that I was shaking when I got out of the shower. I shaved closely and then sat down in front of the bathroom mirror. I stepped into my new white panties and I was immediately engulfed in a warm, erotic rush. I slid my pantyhose over the panties and couldn't believe the feeling. It seems odd now, but while I had worn pantyhose all those years, panties had never really interested me. I couldn't believe what I'd been missing; they felt wonderful. I then strapped myself into my beautiful white lace bra. It was snug but it felt good. I stuffed the cups with pantyhose and then glided into my exquisite, silky full slip.

I was literally trembling as I did my makeup. I took my time and enjoyed a drink and a cigarette while I made up. I couldn't believe what happened next: I suddenly remembered that I used to watch my mom getting ready to go out for an evening. She would be seated in her slip at her makeup table with a drink and a cigarette— and here I was now: Like mother, like son!

I finished my makeup. It looked good. I took the wig off the wig head and slowly slid it onto my head. I was amazed when I looked at myself in the mirror, for I really did look like a woman. I felt bubbly and giggly and euphoric. It was wonderful.

I took my wig off for just a moment so I could finish dressing. I placed a scarf over my face, just as I read in a women's magazine, to avoid messing my dress when I slid it on. The pink sweater dress fit loosely. I belted it with the pink belt and slipped on my favorite pink high heels. I then placed my wig back on and stood in front of the big mirrors on my closet doors.

I was in heaven. It was a silky bliss. I had no idea that cross-dressing could be this fabulous, or I would have started when I was very young. It was like when I first visited Disneyland when I was seven. I never wanted this feeling to go away. I started rubbing myself through the slippery layers of slip, hose, and panties. I came right away.

I changed into the blue panties and stayed dressed for about another four hours. By then it was close to midnight, and I had to go to work early the next day to start a validation procedure. I sadly undressed and showered. I tried to sleep but images of that night kept going through my head. I got back up and put the blue panties back on along with my bra and slip. I went back to bed and slept like a baby.

TRANSVESTITE HANGOVER

Gilbert's experience sounds wonderful, doesn't it? Well, I guess if you're a CD it does. Nevertheless, there's more to his story:

I woke up five thirty the next morning. After I showered, I noticed that my face was broken out from the cosmetics, and it hurt to shave. I decided to be daring and wear the remaining pair of pink panties under my work clothes. I had never worn pantyhose under my work clothes because my socks slipped down and you could see them. I made sure I wore a pair of thick wool slacks so I wouldn't have to worry about embarrassing panty lines!

I got to work and convened the morning meeting to lay out the assignments for the validation procedure to my six team members. As I walked in front of the group of primarily women, I suddenly felt very ashamed about my masturbatory cross-dressing orgy the night before. The pink lace-trimmed panties clinging to my body only heightened my sense of shame. I was truly embarrassed for myself. My usual sense of maleness had escaped me. I felt like a sissy, and I was ashamed.

I thought that if anyone found out I was a "transvestite" (I could barely admit this to myself) they would laugh at me. I got the procedure started and tried to lose myself in my computer screen. But every time I shifted in my chair I could feel my pink panties. I alternated between having an erection and being overly self-conscious. I kept thinking that everyone knew I was wearing women's underwear and that they were laughing at me behind my back. I wished I could hit the delete key on last night. Lunch finally came and I ran home and took off that damn underwear.

It was another month before I cross-dressed again. The same sense of shame settled over me the next day. I just couldn't reconcile cross-dressing and being a man. The urges were powerful—as was the sense of shame. I felt like I was in a dilemma from which I would never escape.

About a year after I had first dressed, I got into therapy. I feel much better about my cross-dressing these days and belong to a CD support group. But you know what? Just like they say that a gun is not a neutral object, I can tell you that women's clothing is not neutral—it does unimaginable things to a man's psyche when he first starts wearing it. Cross-dressing is not something to take lightly.

When I finally gave in to the fact that I'm a CD, I was finally able to relax about it. I just realized that a part of me is feminine. I even gave my "femme self" a name: Victoria. I've never known anyone by that name, I've just always thought that it sounded so regal. Now that I can let Victoria express herself freely, I'm much happier. My only real concern with cross-dressing is being able to find a woman who can accept and enjoy it with me.

Gilbert's story reveals yet another level of complexity in the CD experience. As a cosmetic CD, he mentions two prominent aspects of contemporary cross-dressing.

THE CD SUPPORT GROUP

The first aspect is that of the CD support group. The past thirty years has seen a proliferation of CD support groups in the Western world. What is a CD support group like? The club I first joined and of which I later served two terms as president, PPOC (Powder Puffs of California), is a good representation of CD support groups. PPOC's membership represents a broad cross-section of the socioeconomic spectrum. The club has strict rules regarding confidentiality and conduct. It is open to wives, girlfriends, and therapists, but not the media or public. All sorts of vendors attend the meetings to offer various goods and services for CDs who don't wish to shop publicly for their needs. PPOC also publishes a monthly newsletter.

PPOC's monthly meeting is held on the third Saturday of each month in a hotel ballroom. Changing rooms are provided for those members who cannot get ready at home. Meeting topics are educational. Our speakers have included therapists, educators, cosmeticians, breast form suppliers, wives, and members with expertise in various aspects of cross-dressing. Anywhere from fifty to ninety CDs attend the meetings. The club holds a yearly four-day convention that attracts people from around the country and overseas.

In the eight years I've been associated with PPOC, the club has helped over 250 men come out of the closet. We call them "first-timers," and, believe me, they're nervous when they make their debut at a PPOC meeting. But eventually they relax and are glad to see that there are other men like them.

The emphasis at PPOC is not on appearance or "passing" but rather on acceptance and support. Because passing for a woman is a feat few CDs can actually achieve, most quit worrying about it once they find a safe and accepting environment in which to express themselves.

Given the inherent difficulties of being a CD, I can't recommend membership in a club strongly enough. A CD club offers support that cannot be found anywhere else. I've discovered in working with CDs that the simple process of socialization itself helps to alleviate the sense of alienation, guilt, and obsession that many feel. The important thing for any CD to realize is that he is not alone—and that's where CD clubs excel, particularly in helping men to come out of their closets and into an environment in which their dignity is affirmed.

Non-CDs who are interested in attending a club meeting should always get permission beforehand or they typically will not be allowed in due to security and confidentiality concerns. Also, permission must be obtained before any photographs are taken.

Many CDs stay in the closet because they simply don't know any other CDs or any safe places to go. How does a CD find out where to go to meet other CDs? Appendix A contains a list of CD clubs. Most welcome wives and girlfriends and usually can provide the names and numbers of therapists in your area if counseling is needed.

THE FEMME SELF

The second aspect that Gilbert touches upon is the prevalent notion within cosmetic cross-dressing that the CD has a femme self. In my mind, this concept is like smoking around gasoline, for it is an invitation to trouble.

The cosmetic CD commonly reports that he feels a heightened sense of well-being and pleasure when he cross-dresses. Masturbation, though certainly not the only element, is an important contribution to the pleasure of cross-dressing. Unfortunately the sense of well-being and eroticism associated with cross-dressing is frequently interpreted by the cosmetic CD to be the essence of the female experience. In fact, this altered state is significant enough for the CD to assume a feminine name to embody and characterize this experience.

Within the CD community, the assumption of a feminine name is understood to be an acknowledgement of a man's femme self. Yet to the degree that the CD equates his femme self with only the positive, altered state he experiences while cross-dressed, he falsifies the female experience.

If we were to ask single, working mothers, for example, if a sense of well-being and sexual pleasure described their lives, we would, in most cases, be smacked for being stupid. The troublesome concept of the femme self also reinforces the idealization of femininity and the demonization of masculinity seen in the cross-dressing community.

My criticisms are not intended to trivialize the CD's experience. Rather, they serve to call attention to the fact that the femme self of the CD is best understood as a celebratory expression of a man temporarily freed from the chains of masculinity.

CDs experience cross-dressing as a profound form of personal liberation, which accounts for the intensely positive feelings cross-dressing engenders. This fact, however, is neither understood nor appreciated by our culture, and, to the degree that the CD himself cannot articulate the essence of his experience (perhaps because it is so embedded in guilt), he incorrectly equates it with being a woman.

It is no wonder, then, that many women find themselves offended by CDs, for these unthinking men, despite their insistence to the contrary, seem to mock women by claiming to be equal to them while cross-dressed. Yet this is not to say that there is any one definitive experience of being a woman, for women themselves do not agree on what it is to be a woman.

I prefer to use the term *female persona* in lieu of *femme self* with respect to the cosmetic CD, as it more accurately conveys what the assumption of a feminine name signifies. For the cosmetic CD, who only occasionally cross-dresses, the use of a feminine name defines an intermittent persona which he uses to embrace femininity.

In terms of our discussion of the evolution of cross-dressing, the femme self of the cosmetic CD is a way of attaining what the fetishist never could. Rather than furtively possessing a mere article that symbolically represents a woman, the cosmetic CD constructs himself in the image of a woman.

The CD's image differs from the fetishist's symbol in the same way that a movie differs from a photograph. This comparison is compelling, for the power of a photograph to arrest the attention is an intriguing metaphor for fetishism. Likewise, the ability of a movie to bring a character to life is a provocative metaphor for cross-dressing.

When the CD begins to dress as his femme self, the feminine clothing and cosmetics trigger psychophysical cues that smooth the CD's transition from the male to the female self. The act of "getting dressed up" is usually a one- or two-hour process that essentially deconstructs, visually and psychologically, the male self and constructs the femme self. The process is distinct from fetish masturbation, in which one's male self remains unchanged. One can begin to see the many psychological advantages offered by having a femme self.

Whereas the conversion from fetishism to transitional fetishism is largely accomplished through therapy or self-insight, the transition from transitional fetishism to cosmetic cross-dressing is realized through socialization with other CDs. The femme self gives the CD an identity and membership within the transgender community. Like a foreign legion of gender, the TG community is full of men who have joined to forget.

What we wish to forget is our masculine selves. Here we are equals in dresses. We are the runaways, escapees, and AWOLs of masculinity. The assumption of the femme self represents a baptism into the society of the transgendered much the same as taking a secret name marks one's initiation into a secret society.

Psychologically the femme self is the focusing of a CD's *need for the feminine*, and *fantasies of the feminine*, onto himself. The CD creates a female persona in order to legitimize his need for the feminine as expressed in cross-dressing. As in fetishism, a woman is still being sought in cosmetic cross-dressing.

The femme self also serves some CDs as a compartmentalized response to masculine failure, fear of homosexuality, or whatever other demons might motivate a particular CD. By having a distinct femme self the CD can psychologically fragment this sometimes troubling aspect of himself. This fragmentation allows the CD to keep his male self intact.

At its worst, the femme self of the cosmetic CD is superficial and utterly self-centered. If CDs display a consistent character flaw, it is that of self-centeredness and indulgence when it comes to cross-dressing. But this is not surprising, for the femme self provides the CD with an enormous amount of self-gratification. In this sense, the femme self of the CD is simply a pleasurized, cosmeticized version of the pursuit of happiness.

Far from being remarkable, the femme self is often a troubling persona that must be constantly accommodated, defended, indulged, scheduled, and financed. I mention the issues of time and money because to cross-dress well is expensive and time-consuming (I speak from personal experience, believe me!). The amount of time and money spent is a direct reflection of the CD's emotional involvement with cross-dressing. It also presents a significant potential for resentment and jealousy on the part of the CD's wife.

The femme self is said to be characterized by a decreased sense of inhibition. This gives the CD a feeling of ease, but at the same time it can lead to unwise behavior. It is reasonable to ask if this decreased sense of inhibition might be the influence of obsession.

THE SHE-MALE

The term *she-male* is commonly used in pornographic books and movies. The she-males featured in the erotic media are typically drag queens or preoperative transsexuals who sport silicone breasts and perform the same acts that female porn stars do—the only difference being that she-males don't need strap-on dildos to penetrate their fellow actors and actresses.

Unlike her video counterpart, however, the typical she-male is not a drag queen or a pre-op transsexual. As I define the term, a she-male is a bisexual cosmetic CD who enjoys his penis tremendously. The she-male would never want to have sexual reassignment surgery, nor would he necessarily want to take female hormones, as they make it difficult to develop and maintain an erection. Female hormones also reduce the intensity and volume of the male orgasm as they atrophy the prostate and testicles.

The typical she-male dresses and works as a man during the day.

He is bisexual, yet only has sex with men while dressed as a woman. The thought of sex mano-a-mano holds little interest to the she-male. My friend Chuck is a she-male who goes by the name Caroline. He recently ran an ad in a pornographic contact magazine that read something like this:

> Submissive, smooth-shaven she-male into black lingerie seeks hung stud for hot motel action. French active, greek passive, into bondage. Will dress like a french maid and serve you on my knees. Hairy men in pantyhose need not reply. Caroline, San Francisco, Code JQ141A.

Allow me to interpret the language of porno ads for the uninitiated: "French" is a euphemism for oral sex; "french active" refers to the active participant in oral sex. "Greek" is a euphemism for anal sex; "greek passive" refers to the passive participant in anal sex. "Hairy men in pantyhose" refers to the fact that Caroline is often contacted by men who want to act out their fetishistic desires with her.

On this point, she recounts an incident in which a traveling salesman answered her ad. They met for drinks. Caroline described him as "a swarthy hunk." They went up to his motel room after a few cocktails. He disappeared into the bathroom for about five minutes only to reappear dressed only in a pair of pantyhose.

"I don't normally mind hair on a man's back, but when he's wearing only a pair of pantyhose it really looks gross," she remarked.

I asked her what the guy in the pantyhose did after coming out of the bathroom.

> He took a joint out of his cigarette pack, lit it, and between hits started to tell me about how much he loved pantyhose. Then he started to jack off inside his pantyhose. It didn't take long before he shot his wad all over the inside of the pantyhose.
>
> I began to laugh. I mean, I was kind of drunk and here was this stoned, hairy guy in a pair of pantyhose with cum all over the front of them. I don't even know what the point of him having me up to his room was. I guess he just wanted to jerk off in front of someone. The whole situation—me dressed like a woman and this cum-soaked businessman in a pair of queen-size pantyhose—just

struck me as hilarious. I imagined it as a great scene for a dark comedy.

Anyway, the guy got really pissed off or embarrassed because I was laughing. He called me a "fucking dick-sucking queen" and told me to get the hell out of his room. I ran out because I was afraid he was going to beat me up. I left his hotel room door wide open so that he would have to close it. I heard it slam as I was making it into the elevator.

After that incident, I decided that I didn't want to play fantasy princess to closet queens anymore. If they want to jack off in pantyhose or girdles, they can just find someone else to do it with. I want to be the girl. I want to be the only one who wears women's clothing in a relationship.

When I'm dressed up I feel like a woman. But when I have sex with a man, I *know* that I'm really a woman. I've always felt like a woman since I was young. I have two older sisters and I've been wearing their clothes ever since I can remember. When they started dating boys I used to get so jealous. I wanted to get all dressed up just like them and have a man make a fuss over me. I felt so guilty for having these feelings, but what could I do? They were my honest feelings.

When I was in high school I hung out with all of the people in theater arts. I dated a very beautiful girl in high school. We used to make out all the time, but I was always left wishing that I was her. She broke up with me right before graduation. I was so depressed and hurt. That's when I started to cross-dress seriously. It was such a nice escape.

In junior college, one of the guys in my theater arts class came on to me after school one day. I had been fantasizing about having sex with a man for a long time. We went over to his apartment and he wanted to have sex. I just couldn't. I knew that I could only do it if I was dressed like a woman. I explained this to him, but he wanted nothing to do with it.

Shortly after that I met an older woman and started dating her. One weekend her parents were away and we went over to their

Virginia Prince, 1948. This is the first professional photograph taken of Virginia, photographer unknown.

Cosmetic cross-dresser and pretender to the throne of England, 1958

Photo *Transvestia* magazine, courtesy Sandy Thomas Publications

An attractive cosmetic CD exhibiting a proper sense of Catholic restraint, 1963

Photo *Transvestia* magazine, courtesy Sandy Thomas Publications

Fur was once an acceptable fashion, as demonstrated by this CD in 1965

Photo *Transvestia* magazine, courtesy Sandy Thomas Publications

The Belle of the Ball, 1961

Photo *Transvestia* magazine, courtesy Sandy Thomas Publications

Virginia Prince, 1962

An elegant CD out for a drink, 1971

Photo *Transvestia* magazine,
courtesy Sandy Thomas Publications

Jo Ann Roberts, Ph.D., founder
of Rennaisance and author
of twenty CD self-help books
and videos, 1995

The beautiful Shenna, 1995

The stunning Dr. Tess is probably the world's sole practicing preoperative transsexual dentist, 1995. Only in America could gender bending and root canals happen together.

Joan, distinguished former Air Force officer, aerospace industry layoff victim, cofounder of PPOC, and owner of the PPOC Trailer Rancho; photo taken in 1995 at the Mobile Home Park Operators Association of America's annual meeting in Tulsa

The captivating Monika Dare in a vinyl dress, demonstrating a tasteful blend of cosmetic cross-dressing and fetish fashion, 1995

Monika Dare in a Chinese silk dress, 1995

Jill, 1995

Photo by Joel Greenberg, Real Faces

A striking double exposure showing the male and female sides of Gordon/Shirley, 1993

Photo by Joel Greenberg, Real Faces

Sandy Thomas, the renowned publisher of CD fantasy literature, 1985

Opposite page:
Parody of 1950s-era
Charles Atlas ad

Courtesy Sandy Thomas
Publications

The fabulous Ms. Rebecca H. Heels, one of the world's foremost
devotees of transvestite/fetish bondage

Photo Ms. Rebecca H. Heels, Versatile Fashions

Ms. Rebecca H. Heels
demonstrating the severe
immobility of her chosen delight

Photo Ms. Rebecca H. Heels,
Versatile Fashions

Ms. Rebecca H. Heels from the rear

Photo Ms. Rebecca H. Heels,
Versatile Fashions

Christina, the notorious "transvestite tornado," 1995

house. We started necking on her parents' bed. Before long she excused herself to "slip into something more comfortable." When she came back she looked stunning. She was wearing a beautiful black baby-doll nightie and high heels. Her makeup and hair looked perfect. She laid on the bed and told me that she was going to make me feel real good.

She went down on me. I had never had a woman do that to me before. I was so turned on, but at the same time I was so jealous. I wanted to be her. I mean, I wanted to be the beautiful woman in lingerie who was going down on a man. I lost my virginity to this older woman, but I also discovered my own irresistible urge to have sex with a man while dressed as a woman.

I think I feel this way because deep down inside I'm really a woman. I don't think I'm gay because I like to have sex with women; I also won't have sex with men unless I'm dressed like a woman. When I'm dressed an entirely different part of me comes to life. I become Caroline when I'm dressed up, and it's natural for Caroline to want to make love to men.

Caroline's first relationship with a man occurred when she was twenty-two. What was it like?

I met David at a bar in the Tenderloin district. He was married with kids in college and was fiftyish. He said he hadn't had sex with his wife in years, but didn't want a divorce. His series of affairs with women left him cold. He told me he once had an experience with a transvestite prostitute in Singapore during his days in the Navy that he found terribly exciting, but that he could never bring himself to repeat the experience until he was much older.

I met him after he had been "checking out the scene" for a few weeks in a bar that is frequented by she-males. We hit it off right away. It felt so natural for me to slip into the feminine role with David emotionally and sexually. The first time we made love I felt like a teenage girl who was losing her virginity to an older man. I guess that's one unique thing about being a she-male: You get to lose your virginity twice!

We wound up meeting once or twice a week at my place for about a year. Our dates were almost always the same. I would put on my hair and face, then slip into a lacy bra, garter belt and stockings, panties, high heels—and put a filmy gown on over it. David would come over and we would have a few drinks and talk. I would then go down on him—he never went down on me—and then he would make love to me, always with a condom of course. The sex was good because David was really hung and knew how to treat me like a woman.

I really didn't mind the limitations of our relationship because I was still feeling this whole thing out emotionally. During the entire time we dated, David never once saw me as a man. Neither of us wanted that to happen.

David would always bring me beautiful lingerie or high heels as gifts. I loved those gifts—especially a gorgeous corset that he bought me when he was in Europe—because they made me feel like such a woman. Our relationship ended when David relocated to Texas for a job promotion. I still see him when he visits San Francisco, but I miss the regular sex. I just haven't met anyone since David that I like enough to get together with regularly. I still date, but I'm very cautious because of AIDS. I guess I'm looking for what every adulteress is—an older, safe, well-to-do married man.

Caroline often barhops with her friend Jennifer (Fred). Unlike Caroline, who has sex with men only while she is cross-dressed, Jennifer has sex only with other cross-dressed men. Jennifer considers herself to be a *transvestite lesbian*. Jennifer's wife, Loretta, a genetic girl (GG), is also bisexual. Loretta prefers to relate to Jennifer rather than Fred because she doesn't like men, so Fred has lived like Jennifer everywhere except at work.

I say "has lived" because now that Fred and Loretta have a child on the way, Loretta, wishing the child to have a proper father, wants Fred to be Fred full-time—at least when he's at home. Fred has become morose over the matter. The poor child will probably grow up to become a tax-and-spend liberal.

THE FEMME SELF AND THE SHE-MALE

The femme self provides the psychological rationale for she-males to indulge in sex with other men without considering it to be homosexual behavior. "I'm not gay because I'm a woman when I have sex with a man," goes the argument of she-males such as Caroline. The basis of this logic is that to be a woman is essentially a self-declaration or a state of mind, either of which can exist independent of anatomy. Does such logic defy biology and rational thought?

It depends. There are two ways of approaching this question. In the first, one could argue that for the she-male to call himself a woman is simply a way to deny his homosexuality, to allow himself to enjoy a taboo behavior by attributing it all to his femme self. In this sense, the femme self is but a psychological ploy that allows for the best of both worlds: A man can enjoy his erection and orgasm while at the same time labeling any of his homosexual behavior as heterosexual. But why stop there? Defining himself as a woman also allows the she-male to even avoid being labeled a cross-dresser. In this case, we would simply be dealing with a heterosexual woman who happens to have an oversize clitoris.

While the rationale of the she-male may seem to be nothing more than a transparent attempt at rationalization, upon closer examination it reveals an interesting form of transvestic metaphysics. The she-male wishes to experience the role of the woman during sex with a man, yet he does not want to become a female. The only way to accomplish this is through the vicarious agency of the femme self.

In the same way that the cosmetic CD interprets the pleasure he derives from cross-dressing as the essence of femininity, the she-male likewise interprets the sensations of man-to-man sex as equivalent to man-to-woman sex. He does this by psychologically translating reality into fantasy via the mechanism of the femme self. The homosexual act is merely a means to an end, namely achieving the imagined experience of being a woman having sex with a man.

The she-male thus takes the willing suspension of disbelief to a new level. But is her suspension of disbelief really any different from what one sees in religion, politics, or love? No, for projecting the self into fantasy and illusion at the expense of reality is an essential feature of human nature. The only reason that the she-male's behavior seems so scandalous is that her experience is alien to most people.

The second option in interpreting the she-male's behavior takes us to the cutting edge of transgenderist thought. In her 1995 book, *The Apartheid of Sex: A Manifesto on the Freedom of Gender,* Martine Rothblatt argues:

> Sexual orientation in the third millennium will evolve toward a unisexual model because "male" or "female" sex types will fade away . . . . When society thinks that genitals dictate sex roles, it is natural to think that one's sex role is forever—the genitals cannot change easily. When society understands that the mind dictates sex roles, it is possible to think that one's sex role is easily alterable—after all, we all change our minds.
>
> It is even possible to redefine one's genitals, temporarily for sex or for a longer term as part of a sexual identity shift. There are persons in the trans-gendered movement who think of their penises as enlarged clitorises, and obtain satisfaction by rubbing rather than penetrating their lovemate. There are persons with vaginas who think of their clitorises as small penises and, often with the help of strap-on dildos, obtain sexual satisfaction by penetrating rather than rubbing their partner.

Rothblatt advances her *paradigm of sexual continuism,* or the idea that male and female form a continuum, as the new way to think about sexuality. In her view, the mind is the all-important aspect of sexuality; the genitals are incidental. Sexual continuism would allow the she-male—or any other man for that matter—to legitimately declare himself a woman since "woman" is a state of mind.

This matter of men who call themselves women—and their justifications for doing so—is a fundamental concern in analyzing crossdressing. Such an assertion raises questions about how culture constructs sexual taboos and gender roles; it also goes to the heart of how transgendered people construct reality.

As we have seen in this chapter, the femme self is a persona that allows the cosmetic CD to express his feminine nature. Although he may feel very much like a woman when cross-dressed, the cosmetic CD knows that he is not a woman. And while the cosmetic CD's feminine nature is very real, its magnitude is not sufficient to compel him to transsexualism. In essence, a cosmetic CD is simply a man who enjoys dressing like a woman.

When a man asserts that he is a woman, however, he makes a quantum leap from cosmetics to core identity. But where does his core identity reside? In reality or fantasy? In the next two chapters we will consider in detail those men who call themselves women.

5

FULL-TIME AND CHEMICAL
CROSS-DRESSERS

When the cosmetic CD washes off his makeup, he goes back to being the same man that he's always been. When the full-time CD washes off her makeup, (s)he goes back to being the woman she's always considered herself to be. I also use the term *chemical CD* to denote the fact that many of the people who comprise the full-time category take female hormones to feminize their male bodies.

Three hurdles separate the girls from the women in the world of cross-dressing: living full time as a woman, taking female hormones, and undergoing sexual reassignment surgery. These hurdles also represent the social divide in the TG community. Full-time CDs tend to look down their noses at part-time CDs. In this chapter we'll meet the three types of CDs who have vaulted these hurdles.

The first type we'll meet is the *transgenderist* (TG). What is the profile of a TG? I define a TG as a man who lives full time in the gender role of a woman. While a TG has had electrolysis to remove facial hair, and perhaps some cosmetic procedures to enhance the feminine lines of her face, she typically doesn't have breast implants. The TG has experimented with female hormones, yet she doesn't take them on an ongoing basis. The TG does not want to undergo sexual reassignment surgery (SRS).

Many TGs are monosexual. This has lead some therapists to conclude that monosexuality is perhaps part of a pathology; others have concluded that the difficulty of finding a mate who can accept a TG is the cause.

The *preoperative transsexual* (pre-op TS) lives full time as a woman, takes female hormones, has had breast implants and other feminizing cosmetic procedures, and undergoes extensive psychological counseling in preparation for SRS. Yet for all of this, the pre-op TS is still on the diving board looking into the deep waters of surgery. The pre-op TS can still turn around and not go through with it.

The final type, the *postoperative transsexual* (post-op TS) has taken the plunge and had her body surgically altered to make it resemble a woman's. The purpose of SRS, as stated by the post-op TS, is to make her body conform to her inner nature, which is that of a woman.

LIVING FULL-TIME AS A WOMAN

Living full time as a woman is quite different from merely adopting a femme self. The femme self of the CD is but a female persona that is expressed during occasional cross-dressing. The CD's femme self is temporal, whereas the transgenderist wishes to establish a permanent and functional identity as a woman. The transsexual further desires to establish a permanent, functional, *and* genital identity as a woman.

Society is quick to ridicule the man who would become a woman. What society may not fully appreciate, however, is the extreme courage it takes for a man to declare before the world his intention to become a woman. It is something of a monastic rite akin to renouncing the world to undertake a pilgrimage in search of truth.

The man who would become a woman is declaring that his true self lies in a land other than the one into which he was born. His pilgrimage requires that he leave the man's life behind him and travel into the foreign realm of womanhood. There, he must face the rejection and criticism of the native-born. He will also be ridiculed and perhaps subject to self-doubt.

The temptation is to give up and return home, a failed man who never found his true nature. But if he faces the trials of the pilgrimage, he will eventually find his true self, and that true self will be a she. With luck this new woman will eventually pass unnoticed into the fabric of her adopted homeland, never again to return to the place of her birth.

THE TRANSGENDERIST

The cosmetic CD only flirts with being a woman. He dresses as a woman only when it pleases him. The CDs we've looked at closely so far do not live full time as women. To do so requires a shift in a CD's psyche in which he decides that he is more like a woman than a man. The process of living as a woman allows a CD to determine if he's truly serious about being a woman.

The risks of living full time as a woman are emotional and financial. The TG who is living as a woman may not be able to find satisfactory employment, particularly if he cannot pass for a woman. Moreover, it is almost impossible for the TG to find romance with a genetic woman. Rare indeed would be the woman who would want to date, let alone marry, a man who lives full time in the role of a woman. Unless a TG is gay or bisexual and can find a man who wants to date her, there is little or no possibility of romance.

Sharon (Glen) has dressed and lived full time as a woman for years, yet she doesn't want to have sexual reassignment surgery. Why? Let's have Sharon tell you about her lifestyle:

> First of all, I'm not a TS. I consider myself to be feminine, and I believe that femininity is not a matter of anatomy. I have lesbian friends who are definitely not feminine. Likewise, I am definitely not masculine. The issue for the transgenderist is just that: gender. I am a male who wishes to adopt a feminine gender role. A TS, on the other hand, wants to be both feminine *and* female. The desire to live in the opposite gender is the essence of transgenderism, whereas the desire live as the opposite sex is the essence of transsexualism.
>
> I also don't consider myself be a CD. Why? First of all, CDs only

dress part of the time. For them it's all about the clothes, the cosmetics, and the hair. CDs aren't into the psychological aspects of femininity so much as they're into getting off on the clothes, the wigs, and the cosmetics.

When I was nineteen and first started dressing, I was just into the clothes. I would get all dolled up on Saturday night and get off on the perfume, the stockings, and the heels. Femininity started getting more serious for me when I was about twenty-two. My weekend dressing started to carry over to the weekdays. Pretty soon I realized that it wasn't just for fun anymore—I really did have a serious need to dress and act in a feminine manner all of the time.

Of course this interfered with my job, especially when I started taking female hormones. I would have these hormonal mood swings at work. I began to hate having to get up every morning and face the world as a man. Life always seemed so much easier and less stressful when I could begin and end the day as a woman.

My girlfriend and I broke up shortly after I started taking hormones because she couldn't handle the situation. She said she wasn't sure who I was anymore and didn't want to be involved with a woman. I can't blame her for that. The only thing I ever got pissed off at her about was when she moved out and took all of our good cosmetics. I mean, she took the Lancome and left me with the Cover Girl crap. She also took some of my really good lingerie. Oh, well, that's a woman for you.

Anyway, right after my breakup I met Rachel, another TG who was in the same situation. Rachel moved into my apartment to split expenses and share the misery. I quickly found out that Rachel was turning tricks on the side to support herself. I guess I could've lived with that because she wasn't involved with drugs. The problem was that she wanted to have her clients up to my apartment.

One day I walked into the apartment and there was Rachel dressed in *my* little blue baby-doll nightie and white stockings, and some guy is screwing her while she's going down on another guy— right on my leather sofa! Imagine the nerve, Rachel's there doing a ménage à trois in my house, on my sofa—and to top it off she's wearing my favorite baby-doll nightie! And then the bitch acted like I wasn't even there. She ignored me and kept right on with her work.

After this episode I told her to move out. That was about eight years ago. After Rachel I went through a series of roommates. Cross-dressers, transsexuals, gay men, lesbians—you name it and I've lived with one of them—and I have to tell you that it seems like people who are into sexual trips are all irresponsible and self-absorbed. I mean, I'm into my thing but I would never rip anyone off like I've been ripped off. I consider myself just another person trying to scrape by.

How does Sharon, a man who dresses and lives like a woman on a full-time basis, manage to make a living?

One of the biggest problems I have in life is finding steady employment. It's hard to find a company that will hire me. To be honest, I don't pass flawlessly as a woman. Although I've never had much of a beard, I still have a masculine frame and large hands. Also, I just don't care to lie about who I am. I always tell a prospective employer the truth and it usually winds up costing me the job.

I've worked as free-lance writer, a house-sitter, a painter, a part-time bartender, and just about anything else I can do, legally, to get money. I have to tell you, I got caught up in this thing before I really realized what was happening. When I was young I never thought about what a TG was supposed to do to make a living—especially as she got older. I always thought that being able to live full time as a woman would be the solution to my problems. I guess it solved one need, but all of life's other problems are still there.

Despite the obstacles I face, I wouldn't go back to my old lifestyle where I lived full time as a man. I just wasn't happy having to be a man, and cross-dressing only part of the time was unsatisfying. I feel more comfortable as Sharon than I did as Glen. Although I've retained many of the positive attributes of Glen, I consider myself to primarily be Sharon.

Sharon is more than a mere persona that I created. People think that CDs or TGs just make up these female characters and names. The outside world finds it so hard to believe that a man can have an authentic feminine identity and that this identity is real. Sharon has a history; it is mine. She was born when I was born. The only thing I ever had to do was acknowledge her reality and give her a name.

I know this sounds terribly schizophrenic, but it's really not. The convention of language forces me to talk about the parts of my overall identity as if they were separate persons, but they're not. When I speak of Sharon, I am speaking of a very ordinary, everyday part of myself. I guess if I'm guilty of anything, it's referring to my feminine self in the third person when trying to explain who I am. So forgive me my grammatic indiscretions, but never accuse me of schizophrenia.

Sharon has paid a high price to live as a woman. What sort of inner necessity motivates her behavior? Wouldn't it be easier if she just hung up her heels and went back to being Glen? "I've thought about going back to living as a man," Sharon confides, "but to do so would negate everything I've tried to become, everything I've tried to do with my life. I guess I've always had this need to be true to myself. If no one else understands it, then so be it. I do what I do because it keeps me sane, it makes me happy, and I feel at home in my female identity."

And what about intimate relationships? Is Sharon gay?

I don't have sex with men. I like women. Period. Sexually I call myself a "transgendered lesbian." This means that I'm a transgendered woman who is turned on by genetic women. I sort of have a girlfriend, I mean she's a lesbian who lives with another woman, but we get together occasionally. Most people roll their eyes when I start to explain all of this; it's not easy for an outsider to make sense of transgenderism.

Ironically, Sharon's life is much like that of any other single woman who lacks job skills: It has very little to do with sex or glamour and has almost everything to do with a lack of resources. Of course Sharon doesn't have to contend with single parenthood, but she does face a lack of medical insurance, itinerant jobs, no savings, lowered expectations, and the prospect of a bleak retirement. Would she have it any better as a man? In our post–cold war economy she probably wouldn't, for unskilled men don't fare well either.

Once the eroticism has been factored out of cross-dressing, it's just another lifestyle. It's different, but it's not exempt from the pressures and challenges of life. In this sense, CDs are no more than ordinary people who prefer to adopt the appearance of the opposite sex. Other than that they pay taxes, have children, get divorced, work, face financial and emotional problems, and suffer life's pain like everyone else.

THE TRANSSEXUAL, BOTH PRE- AND POSTOPERATIVE

To illustrate the visceral wallop packed by the topic of transsexualism, it is useful to recall the Christine Jorgensen story. While Christine Jorgensen was not the first male to undergo sexual reassignment surgery—the Danish painter Einar Wegener had the operation in 1933 and changed his name to Lili Elbe—she was the first transsexual to receive worldwide publicity.

The story hit the news in 1950. It was shocking for Americans to discover that a U.S. soldier, the symbol of all that was masculine, would become a woman. Clergymen denounced transsexualism from the pulpit as an offense against God and nature. The medical community in the United States was plunged into a debate over the ethics of such a procedure. There was a deep ambivalence over transsexualism. On the one hand, the surgery was yet another demonstration of the seemingly limitless power of science to accomplish whatever the human mind could dream. On the other hand, people despised the surgery because they believed that it intruded upon the domain of God. Many also felt that it corrupted medicine to cater to the perverted desires of sick and immoral men.

Upon reading the description of the surgery in the newspapers, there was a national male recoil into deep castration anxiety. An older non-CD acquaintance of mine, in recalling his reaction to the Christine Jorgensen story, remarked, "The thought of getting my balls cut off was unthinkable enough. But what really made me cringe was the idea of getting my dick sliced off. Jesus! What kind of man would let a doctor do that to him!" This same revulsion is felt today when men consider transsexualism. After all, what kind of man would submit to having his "dick sliced off"?

AN OVERVIEW OF TRANSSEXUALISM

Despite its sensationalistic nature, sexual reassignment surgery has become an unremarkable medical procedure available to any man or woman who desires it. Before we meet our pre- and post-op transsexuals, it will be informative to first examine the psychological, medical, and financial aspects involved in male-to-female transsexualism. This overview is important in understanding the tremendous hurdles the transsexual must vault if (s)he is to realize the woman within.

Although CDs and transsexuals share the common element of women's clothing, they are vastly different in psychological terms. The transsexual feels a repugnance toward his male genitals and body that the CD does not. The TS truly feels that "she" is a woman trapped in a man's body, whereas the CD is, for the most part, comfortable with being a male.

How does one become a TS? There are two paths. The first is evolutionary. A CD, for example, can begin life as a fetishist, progress to full-time cross-dressing, and then start flirting with the idea of becoming a transsexual. Certain other men, however, experience no evolutionary process; they come into the world with the feeling that they were born in the wrong body.

While the born TS goes through a period of cross-dressing, there is an intensity and insistence on femininity which is absent in the normal CD. Born transsexuals typically declare their true feelings at an early age and consequently pursue sexual reassignment surgery in their early twenties. The evolutionary TS, on the other hand, often doesn't embark on the road to transsexualism until later in life, usually in his late thirties or early forties.

An evolutionary TS goes through an extraordinary inner struggle as his male identity, and often his marriage, breaks down. Femininity begins to take on a reality and a sense of permanence that is unshakable and undeniable. No longer a game, cross-dressing becomes the chrysalis from which a new woman will emerge.

What are some of the other differences between CDs and transsexuals? While many CDs have their beards and body hair removed by waxing and electrolysis, all transsexuals do. But this is superficial. Taking female hormones marks the first real dividing line between the CD and the TS. While a CD or a transgenderist may experiment with female hormones, he usually discontinues them when he starts to lose his ability to have an erection. The TS, however, will continue to take the hormones because she wants a feminine appearance more than she wants an erection.

Breast implants mark the second line of demarcation between CDs and transsexuals. Because they require an expensive surgical procedure, most CDs avoid them. For the TS, breasts are too important a feminine signature not to possess—even with the risks of connective-tissue disease associated with implants. Plastic surgery to feminize the face, vocal cord surgery to raise the pitch of the voice, silicone implants into the cheeks, and the tattooing of eyeliner and lipliner onto the face are among the procedures transsexuals undergo that CDs almost never undertake.

As an aside, a drag queen might also get breast implants and undergo other cosmetic surgical procedures to enhance her femininity. At that point, the drag queen will start to live full time as a woman. Although the drag queen may be identical in outward appearance to a preoperative transsexual, there is a decided psychological difference between the two. The term *preoperative transsexual* should be taken advisedly, for there exists a class of men who claim the status, yet have no intention of ultimately having the surgery.

Is it easy to become a TS? Absolutely not. In America, there is a set of psychological and medical processes to be undergone before sexual reassignment surgery can take place. The first is the requirement to live full time as a woman for at least a year to see if the person can make a living and adapt to life as a woman. There are also postoperative job questions, family relationships, arranging the cost of the surgery, and other vital issues to handle before making the change.

Dallas Denny, a post-op TS and founder of AEGIS (American Educational Gender Information Service), is a leading authority on the topic of transsexualism. When asked about the costs of transsexualism, Denny replies that one must first look not at the dollars, but at the indirect costs.

She cites the first indirect cost of transsexualism as the loss of marriage. When a man decides to become a woman he can kiss his marriage goodbye: Medical authorities insist that a divorce occur before the surgery can be performed. (But most wives of pre-op transsexuals file for divorce anyway as they do not want to be married to another woman.) Furthermore, an ex-wife may contest visiting rights because she fears that exposing the children to their father's sexual reassignment will be too traumatic.

Along with a divorce comes the loss of marital assets and the possible added burden of alimony and child support. For a pre-op TS, this financial responsibility is compounded by the second indirect cost: loss of job or career. Most employers do not favor the idea of having a pre-op TS "transition" on the job. Legally or not, an employer is likely to consider a pre-op TS a liability in terms of health insurance, emotional stability, and overall reliability. Moreover, if a pre-op TS loses her job, she will probably be hard pressed to find another.

The next indirect cost is that of social ostracism. The family of a pre-op TS may turn away from her. Parents and siblings may find the fact that their son or brother wants to become a woman embarrassing, maddening, or intolerable. The same holds true of the friends the pre-op may have had prior to making the decision to pursue sexual reassignment. Friends may find friendship with a pre-op TS too embarrassing to maintain: How will they explain the relationship? Will others think they are gay or somehow perverted by virtue of association?

Dallas Denny stresses that managing the process of sexual reassignment is critical. There is an average three-year period from the time the pre-op begins counseling until the surgery is completed. During this time there must be preparation for the change. Financial and career planning must be undertaken. Family relationships must be renegotiated. A new support network of friends, therapist, and peers needs to be developed.

THE DIRECT COSTS

The process of sexual reassignment surgery begins with counseling. Counseling is mandated by medical authorities before even female hormones can be taken and runs until well after the surgery is completed. The cost of this counseling is from $50 to $100 per hour, depending upon the program. Several private programs throughout the United States specialize in transsexualism. Their primary purpose is to screen out those who are not truly transsexuals, and to assist those who are to transition. A TS spends about four hours a month in a typical program. Monthly group workshops that can cost from $25 to $100 are also available in some programs.

Dallas Denny remarks that only one in ten people who begin a TS program actually undergo the surgery. The reasons for dropping out include fear, health problems that prevent the administration of female hormones or the surgery, and lack of money.

While some transsexuals are born with feminine features, most need some cosmetic surgery to feminize the appearance. Breast implantation is usually undertaken early in the process of therapy as the presence of breasts adds to the psychological well-being of the pre-op TS. While common cosmetic procedures such as rhinoplasty (the ever popular "nose job") or face-lifts are undergone by transsexuals for the usual reasons of improving overall appearance, specialized procedures such as the tracheal shave—in which the male adam's apple is shaved to give the throat a feminine line—and cheekbone implants are unique to the TS. Hair flap and scalp reduction procedures are popular among transsexuals to eliminate male pattern baldness.

One interesting type of cosmetic surgery undertaken by transsexuals employs a technique in which bone is ground down to reduce brow ridges and male chin contours. Collagen injections into the lips can also be had at an average of $150 each. (Such injections must be periodically refreshed.)

Electrolysis is needed to remove the male beard. Depending upon the heaviness of the beard, removal can take from 100 to 300 hours at an average cost of $50 per hour. The skill of the electrologist is critical. While there is always some regrowth with electrolysis, poor electrolysis can result in pitting of the skin and excessive beard regrowth that makes the procedure still more costly.

The next direct cost is female hormone administration, which includes biannual medical monitoring to ensure that blood and organ functions are not being adversely affected. Female hormones are taken orally on a twenty-eight-day cycle with five days off—similar to birth control pills.

An initial visit to an endocrinologist costs about $250 plus lab work. Follow-up visits typically occur in six-month intervals at around $100 per visit plus lab work. The cost of the hormones varies depending upon what types and dosages are being administered. In addition to antiandrogen drugs, a program of female hormones usually includes either synthetic or natural estrogen and progesterone.

Female hormones feminize the male body by softening the skin, reducing the growth of body hair, broadening the hips, and enlarging the breasts and nipples. Although they are not classed as mood-altering drugs, female hormones can dramatically alter mood by reducing aggression, increasing the sensitivity of the breasts, and heightening emotional states. The changes brought about by these powerful hormones help the TS to look and feel more like a woman.

The risks incurred by a male who takes female hormones include liver disease, breast and liver cancer, brain tumors, strokes, and blood clots (which can be lethal if they lodge in the brain or lungs). These risks increase dramatically if one drinks alcohol, smokes, or uses drugs not approved by an endrocrinologist.

Some drag queens, transgenderists, and transsexuals use illegally purchased hormones without medical supervision. This practice is extremely dangerous and can result in serious illness or death. Female hormones can be legally administered to a male only by a medical doctor upon the recommendation of a board-certified therapist. Under a doctor's supervision, the use of female hormones is a fairly safe and effective way to feminize the male body. However, a male should always first have a complete medical screening to determine if he is a suitable candidate for female hormones.

Sexual reassignment surgery costs between $6,000 and $15,000. A typical surgery begins by removing the testicles, but not the scrotum itself. The penis is then bisected and its interior bodies removed. The skin of the penis and the scrotum are then inverted and pushed into the natural cavity at the bottom of the abdomen.

The inverted scrotal skin is used to construct the labia while the inverted penile skin is used to form the vaginal walls. The erectile tissue of the glans, or the "head" of the penis, is used to construct the cervix. A clitoris is formed from tissue in the perineum. Given the supreme importance of urination, the proper modification and routing of the urethra is the most critical aspect of reassignment surgery. It is not necessary to remove the prostate, which by this point has long since atrophied and stopped functioning due to the effects of female hormones. The surgery lasts between three and six hours, and most post-op transsexuals are back to work within thirty days.

It is commonly believed that sexual reassignment surgery results in the loss of ability to have an orgasm, and that the surgically constructed vagina cannot lubricate itself. Attempts to improve orgasmic sensation have reportedly been successful in the clitoral area. Also, vaginal lubrication has been achieved by grafting a section of the lower intestine—which is always lubricating—onto the vaginal wall.

While the post-op TS will never experience sexual sensations identical to those of a born woman, highly pleasurable sensations are nevertheless generated by the constructed vagina. Most transsexuals report that an emotional relationship with a man and the "feeling of a man being in them" are more than sufficient. However, some male-to-female transsexuals are lesbian and have no desire to be with men. A TS I know remarked to me that although she now has a vagina, she still prefers anal sex. "I always enjoyed it before my change," she noted, "and I see no reason to give it up just because I now have a vagina."

A PREOPERATIVE TRANSSEXUAL

Stephanie (Curt), a pre-op TS, is saving up money for sexual reassignment surgery but is still unsure whether she can actually go through with it. Stephanie is in a mandated one-year program in which she must live and work full time as a woman to find out whether she can handle life as a permanent woman. The medical establishment in the United States requires this trial period prior to allowing a TS to undergo SRS. However, a pre-op TS can go to Mexico for the surgery. It is cheaper in Mexico—but the chances of postoperative complications are higher. Stephanie explains her life this way:

I feel like I'm living in the shadows between two worlds. I'm neither a man nor a woman. While I live full time as a woman, while I consider myself to be a woman, I wake up every day to look at a penis that I truly cannot stand. I've always liked to touch and play with a man's penis, but I've never been able to stand the sight of my own. It will be such a relief to be rid of it. I daydream that I'll wake up after the surgery, pull the sheets back, and see a beautiful female body.

I remember the first time that I shaved my legs it felt so liberating to be rid of my body hair. My legs looked so smooth, so shapely, so feminine. It felt perfectly natural, but then, being a woman has always felt so natural to me. That's why I'm going through this process. I want to make my body reflect the woman that I am spiritually and emotionally.

I knew from early childhood that I was supposed to be a girl. It was such a tremendous disappointment to be a boy. My mama use to hold me close to her. I would lay my head on her breast and imagine myself disappearing into her warm, safe, loving heart. I'm inseparable from my mother. My therapist tells me that this closeness is almost a cliché among transsexuals, and that I need to see myself as a distinct person. But my mother has always been there for me— she always understood that I was a different sort of boy.

Growing up was torturous for me. I wasn't really gay, for when I was with another boy I always imagined myself being a girl. I hated high school because everyone called me gay and made fun of me. The minute I graduated high school in 1993 I decided that I was through being a male and that I was going to become a woman no matter what it took.

After talking things over with my mother, she decided that I could use therapy. In exchange for my going to counseling, she allowed me to live as a woman at our house. I was lucky in that my mother helped me to find a therapist who specialized in gender issues; I was in a program for preoperative transsexuals within a year. Just to be around other people like myself was such a relief.

My biggest problem is that of money. When I realized how much it cost to go through the change, I was overwhelmed. I began to see why some pre-ops turn to prostitution. No one will give them work and they're just so desperate to have the change that they'll do anything. I'll never do that. I have a job as a phone sex actress. It pays pretty good if you're willing to work. I like the late hours because I'm a night person. The job lets me take the calls at my house, so it's very convenient.

It would be so much easier if I could find a rich man to marry, but it's not like there are even that many guys who want to marry a TS, let alone date one. I've dated a bunch of guys, but none of them seem real interested in a commitment. It seems like most of them turn out to be woman-haters who just want a pretty, feminine boy. My only serious boyfriend said he could never marry me if I went through with the change.

Stephanie has a difficult road ahead of her and knows it. She's decided to postpone her change until after she gets her cosmetology license. At least then, she reasons, she'll have a way to support herself.

Some in the transgender community point out that there are nonoperative transsexuals. I don't list this category in my eleven types of CDs because I consider the nonoperative transsexual to be essentially a transgenderist. However, I did want to mention the type to give yet another example of the nuances one encounters within transgenderism. Nonoperative transsexuals are those who would have the surgery but are prevented from doing so by limitations of money, health, or family.

In our next section, we'll meet a postoperative TS. I chose to discuss this particular person because she is so well adjusted—but she didn't start out that way. Karen's is an inspiring story of how a man struggled to become a woman and became a better person for it.

A POSTOPERATIVE TRANSSEXUAL

When my friend Lloyd (Karen) was growing up he didn't just want to be like a woman, he wanted to be a woman. How badly did he want to? Lloyd was institutionalized for a short time in his teens when, after getting high on crack, he mutilated his hated male genitals with a kitchen knife. After leading a tortured existence in his twenties, Lloyd kicked drugs and got into a program for transsexuals that changed his life for the better. Having just completed sexual reassignment surgery, Karen is now legally a woman.

Going through the long process that culminates in sexual reassignment surgery, if I can use an ironic phrase, is such a Herculean undertaking. The first thing everyone always asks me is if sexual reassignment surgery hurts. In my case, it didn't hurt any worse than my appendectomy. The next thing people always ask me is what it costs. It costs a lot. I figure that I spent well over $40,000 in the four years leading up to my surgery. The big question that everybody wants answered, yet nobody dares to ask, is "Does your vagina look real?" It does. It's virtually indistinguishable from a born woman's.

Was the surgery worth it? Yes, yes, yes. Unlike some of my friends, I have absolutely no regrets. I love being a woman and have never once missed being a man. Being a woman has always been an emotional thing for me. It was never about the clothes per se, although I do love clothes.

If there is a hard part about being a post-op TS, it's trying to find my place in the world. I really don't want to stay in the transgendered community because I'm no longer a transgenderist—I'm a woman. I look at my life in the TG community as time spent in a cocoon: I was metamorphosing from a male into a female. But now that I'm out of the cocoon, I'm not so willing to go back and visit. Besides, I'll never find a man to settle down with in the TG community because all the men there want to be women.

How do I deal with the issue of telling a man that I'm a post-op? I have to be very careful obviously. I never date anyone at school because nobody there knows about my past, and I don't want that to change. When I meet a man, I'll usually tell him before we get very involved. It saves us both a lot of trouble that way. Sometimes when I tell a man, it's like *The Crying Game:* He becomes violently ill and just cannot believe it. Most of the time, though, men are polite but firm in letting me know if they're not interested.

It's funny that a man can love a person he thinks is a woman, but the minute he finds out that she used to be a man, everything changes. I can understand a man's reaction, but it is nevertheless interesting to see how love is often based on belief and appearances rather than on a deep, heartfelt caring about another person. I've had to learn some hard lessons about love, rejection, and human nature in becoming a woman.

I've dated two men who said that they didn't care about my past. But when it came time to become committed, they both backed away. I could sense that they were uncertain about their feelings. Still, I know three post-ops who have married and settled into "normal" lives, so I don't worry about my chances. What I want more than anything else is just to fade into the woodwork and get on with my life. Really, I'm just like any other person who had an operation that helped her lead a normal life. Other than the fact of my operation, I'm a regular person with all of the same dreams, hopes, and aspirations as anyone else.

When I was a child I always wanted to be a chef in an elegant restaurant, just like my father. I'm now in school to do just that. Hopefully, I'll be one of the world's great chefs one of these days. The thing about food is that no one ever asks about the sex of the chef. Food, more so than any other artistic medium, allows you to create without any emphasis on sex or gender. I can enjoy my passion for cooking without regard to my past. There are no complications for me in the kitchen, there is only the hectic pace of cooking.

Karen has made a healthy transition from man to woman. She is fortunate, for many postoperative transsexuals continue to suffer emotional problems following surgery. The preoperative period is critical because it emphasizes counseling and the real-world problems of transitioning. The preoperative period also teaches transsexuals that the struggles of living will not go away simply because they are changing their sex. If anything, life will become more of a challenge. If you want more information about transsexuals, you can contact AEGIS (the American Educational Gender Information Service). The phone number and address appear in Appendix A.

CROSS-DRESSING: THE SPIRIT VERSUS THE FLESH

Transsexuals and transgenderists don't always get along with cosmetic CDs. Within the TG community, struggles often erupt between the part-timers and full-timers. I tend to think of these struggles in terms of a battle between spirit and flesh. Because most of those who live full time as women have so much more invested in the practical and political outcome of the TG movement, they are wont to lecture those who are into the lifestyle only for the part-time pleasures it brings. These *dowagers of transgenderism,* as I call them, often decry the emphasis that many in the cosmetic CD community place upon partying, wearing sexy clothing, and eroticism in general.

Such a dour attitude strikes me as strange, even hypocritical in what is, after all, a highly sexual behavior. Isn't it odd that one group of CDs would tell another that this behavior should be about propriety, introspection, and decency? While I promote the ideal of personal responsibility, I still assert that if a guy can't enjoy himself when he's dressed like a woman, then what's the point?

A particularly infamous incident in the CD community in late 1992 illustrates this struggle between spirit and flesh. It seems that a preoperative transsexual went skinny-dipping in the pool of a hotel in which the conservative wing of the TG community was holding its annual convention. The skinny-dipper was observed by some hotel guests who were not there for the convention. They were no doubt shocked by seeing three buoyant appendages where there should have been only one or two. The incredulous guests complained bitterly to the hotel, which in turn threatened to eject the CD convention.

The dowagers went ballistic. They excoriated those they felt were less than serious for jeopardizing the well-being of the community with such antics. They had a point, though, for the skinny-dipping offender risked getting the group thrown out of a hotel in which they had staged meetings for years.

Still, I felt that the dowagers overreacted with a barrage of harsh generalizations against the liberal elements of the community. Being one of the errant "California girls" who was supposedly responsible for such misdeeds, I wrote the following response in the February 1993 edition of "The TV Social Register":

INFLATABLE TV LOVE DOLLS
& THE SOCIO-ERECTOGRAPH

Here's another item that's sure to upset the transgendered morality police. While patrolling the local adult bookstores recently—I do this to keep informed of the latest perversions so that I may protect "my girls" in PPOC from such things—I saw an inflatable "TV Love Doll." The doll was advertised as having beautiful breasts and what I will tastefully term a "rigid protuberance."

Imagine that, a blow-up TV love doll! Well, I guess it just goes to show that the CD movement has really made an impact on culture when blow-up TV love dolls are available to the masses. Despite the seeming absurdity of this latest development in love-doll technology, it nevertheless serves to illustrate what I see as a fundamental disagreement within the CD community.

On the one hand, we have the transgendered morality police who would like to have a sanitized, sexless, and homogeneous form of cross-dressing that equates to having CDs be "polite company" and not offend those in the outside world with displays of unseemly behavior. Circumspect behavior is deemed necessary to earn the respect of the secular world. Those who subscribe to the "polite" school of cross-dressing would never go into a dirty book store, let alone purchase a TV love doll.

On the other hand, there are many long-term CDs, myself included, who are blatantly and unabashedly sexual and who could care less what the world thinks. Such denizens of lewdness would not only buy a TV love doll, but they would no doubt bring their new plastic love slave to a PPOC meeting. The only real question in my mind, given PPOC's dire financial condition, is whether we should charge our inflatable friends an admission fee.

So who is right and who is wrong? Is propriety or titillation the correct response to cross-dressing? Must we seek to please the world by appearing demure at all times, or do we stand defiant before the world in our six-inch spike heels and frilly rubber corsets?

I think it depends upon whether one interprets cross-dressing as primarily a sexual issue or a social activity. This distinction is important—because it goes to the heart of the disagreement between the warring factions of the CD community. Yet even this distinction is flawed in that it presumes that socially oriented CDs have somehow filtered the sexuality out of their cross-dressing. Likewise, it assumes that sexually oriented CDs have no important social interaction with their peers.

Therefore, it becomes apparent that cross-dressing is neither exclusively social or sexual. Indeed, the social and the sexual exist in a ratio proportionate to individual preference. And to the degree that we can recognize and accept the preference of others for either the thrill of the lace or the fellowship of good company, we will all be better off.

But, Dr. Sanhjay, you ask, how can I do this? How can I determine just where another CD stands in terms of the social or the sexual? Well, it's quite simple when you use my new evaluative tool, which I call the Sanhjay Socio-Erectograph (SSEG). This tool is an alphanumeric X/Y graph in which X stands for an individual's degree of erectile response to women's clothing and Y stands for an individual's degree of socialization:

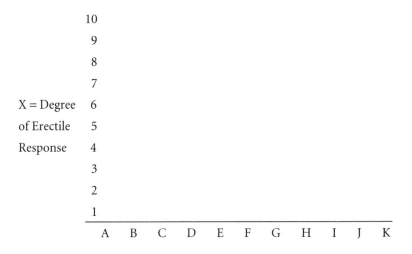

Y = Degree of Socialization

To determine the degree of erectile response, all one need do is ask, "How big a throb do I get from women's clothing?" A rating of 1 suggests someone who cross-dresses like his grandmother, whereas a rating of 10 typifies someone who, shall we say, "loses it" while looking at pantyhose ads in the newspaper. In terms of degree of socialization, a rating of A indicates a person who is deeply closeted, while a rating of K describes the person who is steeped in cross-dressing society.

When we combine the sexual and social scores, we come up with an alpha-numeric rating similar to that which was used by the Selective Service. Fortunately, an adverse rating on our chart won't keep you from serving in the Queen's army.

In the interest of applied research, I can offer some highly presumptuous examples of how the SSEG is used, based on analyzing actual people in our community. Take Tanya P., for example. Now Tanya is obviously past the stage of drooling over pantyhose ads in the newspaper. So her erectile response might be a 3. On the other hand, Tanya is a highly socialized creature and rates a K. Thus she a 3K.

Mary L., judging from her ads and photos in "contact" magazines, is a supercharged sexual vixen and so easily rates a 10. She is also at the hub of CD society, though not to the same degree as Tanya, and so rates a J. Mary's combined rating is 10J.

Now we can interpret a rating of 10J or 3K as either self-actualizing or self-destructive, depending upon how one regards Tanya or Mary. You see, the beauty of the SSEG is that it offers a seemingly objective diagnosis whose interpretation is completely subjective. In this sense, the SSEG comes frighteningly close to functioning as an actual psychiatric device. This is brilliant, is it not? One can begin to see why I have come to possess such awesome power and influence in the CD community!

What about Justine Sahnjay and the SSEG? To begin with, I admit to perspiring a little over pantyhose ads, so I'm a sexual 7. However, I only get out dressed these days to attend PPOC meetings and ride in parades, so I'm a social C. Thus, I'm a 7C.

What about others in our community? Marissa S. is a definite 1J: sensible shoes, jogging outfits, no fetish elements in her wardrobe, and a ubiquitous social presence. Sue S. is a classic 5H: black lace thong underwear and bra hidden under a matronly society-woman exterior. Barb Henderson, a real girl, doesn't cross-dress, and so I can't rate her. However, Vicki R., another real girl, has cross-dressed at our conventions, and, judging her on the SSEG, she rates a 6F. Take a moment now and rate yourself—and remember, don't lie, because I'm watching you very closely.

What begins to emerge as we use the SSEG is a recognition that the CD community exists within a vast range of social and sexual behavior. In view of our differences, can we ever get along? This question will have to wait until next month when I discuss the matter of "Social Responsibility-Versus-Fantasy and Hormonal Urgency." Until then, consider this question: "Should I fondle my TV love doll in the parking lot outside of the PPOC meeting, or do I wait until I'm inside behind closed doors?"

This column was written to make the point that the CD community needs to be more tolerant of its own diversity. My effort was largely misunderstood by the dowagers, who branded me a smart-ass. I half expected this reaction, and I still secretly suspect that it arose because none of them look as good in red velvet as I do. One lesson for us in all of this is that fashion, beauty, and cross-dressing carry risks that cannot be ignored.

6

CAN A MAN BECOME A WOMAN?

Cross-dressing is provocative because it is a male interpretation of femininity. Some women find it insulting, believing that only women should be allowed to interpret femininity. More provocative yet is the transsexual notion that a man can *become* a woman, for it implies that there is nothing about womanhood that a man cannot obtain. This aspect of transsexualism is thought by some feminists to be an Orwellian negation of women.

As an adjunct to their vilification of male sexuality, some feminists have characterized male-to-female transsexualism as the male establishment's attempt to use surgically modified men to infiltrate and sabotage feminism. Author Janice Raymond saw an Armageddon against women coming in the form of transsexualism. In *The Transsexual Empire,* her 1979 book that was to rationality what *Plan Nine From Outer Space* was to cinema, she argued for her *transsexual-infiltration* theory by observing that "masculine behavior is notably obtrusive. It is significant that transsexually constructed lesbian-feminists have inserted themselves into positions of importance and/or performance in the feminist community."

In summarizing her overheated conspiracy theory Raymond asked:

Is transsexual surgery a male-defined, male-perpetuated, and male-legitimated mode of happiness? (The female-to-constructed-male transsexual, as I have argued, is in a most definite sense the disguise that obscures the patriarchal character of the transsexual empire.) Can one view the transsexual "solution" as the beginning of a world where men not only dominate women but become women and try to surpass the biological woman and her creative capacities on all levels?

While the idea of marauding Stepford transsexuals usurping women on all levels is truly frightening, how realistic is such a scenario? Is it actually something that women need fear?

Hardly. The number of men who undergo sexual reassignment surgery is minuscule. Moreover, that some misogynistic cabal of powerful men would plot to supplant women by infiltrating their ranks with transsexual agents on a large scale is ludicrous. If such a male conspiracy indeed existed, the easiest way for it to go about destroying feminism would involve the misuse of government power and trumped-up legal charges.

After all, it would be much faster, easier, and cheaper to have feminists' tax returns audited or plant cocaine in their cars than it would be to devise a program to infiltrate their ranks with transsexuals. A male-to-female transsexual, from start to finish, spends upwards of $50,000 and takes from three to ten years to complete the process—which would be far too long and expensive for most male saboteurs.

The transsexual "solution" simply doesn't pencil out on a straight cost-benefits analysis when compared to the other forms of subversion available to men. Furthermore, heterosexual males, being the pigs they are, would undoubtedly prefer to make love to genuine women than to a race of transsexuals with silicone breasts and surgically engineered vaginas. I swear, men are so predictable!

If cross-dressers and transsexuals are threatening, it's not because they pose a danger of launching a coup against women. Rather, it's their seeming attempt to revoke the unique status of women by arguing that men can become women. This attempt to breach the boundaries between the sexes raises important questions about biology, culture, and equality.

In its quest for freedom, transgenderism—like feminism—often stresses these boundaries. In this chapter, I want to examine the ideas, expectations, and experiences that define the boundaries between men and women and ask which should come down and which should remain.

WHAT IS A WOMAN?

One reason that some people are upset when a CD imitates a woman is that cross-dressing pits the emotional needs of the CD against the gender structure of those around him. The CD doesn't fit either the biological or cultural definition of a woman. In his attempt to be like a woman, he is sometimes criticized as someone who "can't accept reality" or who is "trying to be something that he's not."

"You're not a woman, and you'll never be!" is the often echoed, and often angry, criticism leveled at the CD, particularly by his wife or girlfriend. The issue of what a woman is, more so than any other, cuts to the heart of cross-dressing. We must ask what exactly the CD is pursuing.

Is it an appearance, a mood, a feeling? Is the CD chasing his mother, a lover, or a prostitute, or some other female role model? Or, deluded by cultural constructs, is he pursuing a series of artifices that ultimately have nothing to do with women? Indeed, is it ever reasonable for a man to call himself a woman?

This question depends upon our definition of *woman*. To arrive at such a definition, we must examine the context within which the questions of defining women and cross-dressing exist.

SEX, SEXUALITY, AND GENDER

Sex, sexuality, and *gender* are three important terms that must be defined to discuss the questions at hand. When asked to check the box marked SEX on a driver's license application, one checks either MALE or FEMALE. *Sex* in this case is determined by the genitals with which one was born. Persons born with the genital characteristics of both sexes are said to be *intersexed,* a term which has been developed to replace *hermaphrodite.*

With respect to sex, people often forget the noun because the verb is so popular. For instance, for a woman to say, "My *sex* is female," defines her anatomy, while the rest of her statement, "so naturally Senator Packwood wanted to have *sex* with me," describes the verb, in this case the lascivious Packwood's apparently eternal quest.

The sex of individuals also determines reproductive function. Males can inseminate, while females can ovulate, gestate, and lactate. There are other differences between males and females that can be accounted for on the basis of sex. As a generalization, for example, males tend to be aggressive, while females tend to be nurturing.

Sexuality refers to one's sexual behavior and orientation. The three sexual orientations are heterosexual, bisexual, and homosexual. As an aside, within each of these three classes are seen behaviors such as cross-dressing, fetishism, bondage and discipline, and other alternative forms of sexual expression. A CD, for example, can be heterosexual, bisexual, or homosexual.

What does it say about cross-dressing that it can exist within any of the three sexual orientations? That cross-dressing is not dependent upon sexual orientation. This is important to consider, for it eliminates sexual orientation as a cause of cross-dressing.

Gender is distinct from sex or sexuality. *Gender* refers to those culturally learned behaviors and artifacts that are used to define masculinity and femininity. The term *gender role* describes behavior that a culture expects of males and females. Gender informs self-identity, for it helps us to define who and what we are as a man or a woman. In the simplest sense, gender roles dictate that males should be "masculine" and females should be "feminine."

Although sex and gender are different, gender nevertheless flows from sex. The fact of male aggressiveness can lead to a gender expectation that men will be competitive in all areas of life. Likewise, the quality of female nurturing can foster a gender expectation that a woman should sacrifice a career in business to raise children. These are not altogether reasonable assumptions, particularly if expected of a nonaggressive man or a woman who enjoys the business world.

There remains much confusion over the terms *sex, sexuality,* and *gender.* For example, when a male (sex) expresses uncertainty about his masculinity (gender) in our culture, it is a taken as evidence of homosexuality (sexuality). But is the lack of masculine behavior in a male a sure sign of homosexuality?

Of course not. Nonetheless, many people were surprised when it was announced that Jann Wenner, the longtime editor of *Rolling Stone*, had left his wife of many years for a younger man. "He had never acted gay" seemed to be the consensus on Wenner. What such a statement really means is that Wenner had always fulfilled his gender role by acting like a "normal, heterosexual male." Likewise, the occasionally heard jibe, "She seems too feminine be a lesbian" suggests that only masculine women can be lesbian.

Unfortunately, *sexuality* and *gender* are related in the popular mind. Ironically, while a heterosexual can be unfairly accused of homosexuality simply if he dresses or acts in a manner inappropriate to his gender, it is quite possible for the lesbian, gay male, or CD to escape detection simply by adopting culturally accepted gender roles in their everyday lives. Conversely, many of these people purposely defy or exaggerate the conventions of gender to make the point that such conventions are absurd.

FEMINISM AND THE SUPERFICIAL ASPECTS OF GENDER

The feminist movement was born in part as a protest against conventions of gender that required women to remain weak, underpaid, submissive, uncomplaining, and powerless. To combat such gender bias, feminist theory long ago articulated a distinction between *biological* femininity and *constructed* femininity.

Biological femininity, or what I have termed *sex*, is defined as the irreducible reproductive biology of the female: breasts, ovaries, uterus, vagina, pelvic structure, and the essential hormones to make it all function properly. A woman is biologically designed to give birth to children and then to breastfeed and nurture them. Beyond this bare distinction, argues feminism, everything else that culture calls for from women is a matter of gender.

Gender is said to be comprised of behavioral expectations, social rules, and cosmetic dictates, the sum of which add to a cultural identity, or gender role, for women. Feminists have rightly pointed out that gender roles are artificial and unfair. That women should be weak or submissive, that they should make less money for doing the same work as men, are fallacies that deserve no credence.

We can argue that this same distinction applies to men. Beyond men's reproductive biology, everything else called for in men is but a series of behavioral expectations, social rules, and cosmetic dictates. The notion that a man must be strong, aggressive, or competitive is as unfair as insisting that women can only work at menial jobs.

The women's movement has taught us much about the superficiality of what we call masculinity and femininity. Among the classic hypocrisies that feminism has exposed are the notions that dominant men are take-charge while dominant women are bossy; that promiscuous men are playboys while promiscuous women are sluts; that the male bodybuilder is a stud while the woman bodybuilder is a dyke on steroids; and that a man with a younger woman is acceptable while a woman with a younger man only indicates that she is rich and he isn't or that she is playing mother to a neurotic.

There exist many more hypocrisies of gender, among them: A woman who wears cosmetics does so to enhance her beauty, while a man who wears cosmetics is gay; women who want to work with children are maternal, while men who want to work with children are child molesters; nonaggressive women are nice to be around, nonaggressive men are wimps; women can wear dresses to show off their legs, men who do so are transvestites.

During the eighteenth century, European men wore cosmetics, wigs, and high heels, but now only women can wear them—unless they're women of certain religions that prohibit "worldly" trappings such as cosmetics, pantyhose, and high heels. Oddly enough, men "can't" wear panties, but they "can" wear lavender bikini-style nylon underwear—as long as it's made for men. Of course, it is acceptable for members of either sex to wear cotton briefs, so long as men don't ornament theirs with lace or floral prints, for everybody knows that floral prints or lace on male underwear connotes sissiness; it is taken for granted that lace belongs exclusively to women.

Women can wear corsets to rein in their extra pounds and look more shapely, but men aren't supposed to unless they're big, old fat actors. Men can urinate behind a building or a car if they're desperate, but women must never urinate in public. Under certain circumstances a man can spit in public, but a woman dare not, lest she be thought of as a complete and utter pig.

A man can scratch his privates in public, but a woman must only do so privately. Men can walk around without shirts on when it's hot or when they want to show off their muscles, but women have to leave their tops on for "modesty's sake." This restriction, however, is offset by the fact that women can paint their fingernails and men cannot—unless it's a clear coat applied by a manicurist and done against their will.

Finally, what is eyeliner? It is an artifact the use of which our culture has assigned to women. Eyeliner itself is basically colored wax, yet it has symbolic power. While the use of eyeliner might seem to be a trivial example, the mere sight of a man (aside from an entertainer on a stage) wearing eyeliner suggests homosexuality or effeminacy, because no "normal" man would have any good reason to use eyeliner.

Such artifacts as eyeliner and lipstick are used to mark the boundaries between the sexes. The CD interferes with the cultural order of things by using the artifacts of femininity. In crossing the border of masculinity the CD is not merely putting colored wax on his eyelids; he is using the wax to enter into a domain forbidden to men. The CD has the power to disrupt the neat boundaries set by culture. As Majorie Garber astutely observed in her fascinating book *Vested Interests:*

> One of the most consistent and effective functions of the transvestite in culture is to indicate the place of what I call "category crisis," disrupting and calling attention to cultural, social, or aesthetic dissonances. . . . By "category crisis" I mean a failure of definitional distinction, a borderline that becomes permeable. . . .

The CD is a provocateur who sabotages the artifacts of gender that we take so seriously. We assign potent meanings to these artifacts: colored wax is given the power to signify femininity, and when that same wax is used by a man it is given the power to signify sexual deviance.

For most people this is no game; the integrity of culture and identity depend upon the symbolic artifacts of maleness and femaleness. If the line between male and female were destroyed, then the fundamental way we first learn to differentiate among each other might disappear and we would have to rethink all of the symbols, behaviors, and expectations that the culture has assigned to men and women. How would this change our thinking about such things as aggression, submissiveness, child-rearing, income, competence, blond hair, shoes, the color pink, or even eyeliner?

My questions could continue ad infinitum. The point is that many of the ways in which we define men and women are based upon flawed concepts, many of which are horribly outdated, sexist, and discriminatory and derive from social convention, religious prohibition, romance novelists, advertisers, and clothing and cosmetics manufacturers.

The distinction between *one's biological sex* and *culture's gender constructs* enables us to see that masculinity and femininity are essentially artificial. If men and women are to achieve true equality, everything should be up for grabs: miniskirts, boxer shorts, the office of the president of the United States, congressional seats, wearing cosmetics, and having swarms of policemen chase you across state lines as you and your partner-in-crime engage them in a running shoot-out. Now that the walls are coming down, hairspray and bullets no longer represent different worlds.

We can state with certainty that women cannot *ultimately* be defined by their clothing and cosmetics. To do so would be to argue that women are reducible to such artifacts—and this is exactly what feminism protests. By abandoning this definition, though, do we not open the door to the CD? For is the cultural taboo that prevents the CD from wearing women's clothing and cosmetics valid only to the extent that the woman-as-artifact definition applies?

THE CD AND THE ISSUE OF EQUALITY

If women cannot ultimately be defined by clothing and cosmetics, then the CD is not negating their unique status by dressing like them.

Instead, he could be said to be simply participating with them as an equal in an artifactual arena.

While the women's liberation movement of the sixties was not merely about wearing pants, smoking, or working as a riveter, it nevertheless had its roots in appropriating those artifacts that had once been exclusively associated with masculinity. And while femininity is about more than simply wearing skirts and cosmetics, men, if they are to be truly equal with women, should be free to appropriate the artifacts of femininity.

The feminist might argue that while women want equality with men, they do not want to be men. The same notion applies to the CD. Most CDs do not want to be women; however, they do want the same clothing and cosmetic opportunities as women. Similarly, certain lesbian feminists want the same clothing and cosmetic opportunities as men.

In all fairness, shouldn't the feminist and the CD have the right to dress and act as they please within the limits of the law? After all, everyone else has that right. Conversely, if a man wants to surgically become like a woman, or a woman wants to surgically become like a man, shouldn't he or she have the right to do so?

The CD's argument comes down to the idea that women do not "own" femininity any more than men "own" masculinity. So in the same way that feminism wants to destroy the barriers to male privilege that men have erected, CDs want to destroy the barriers to female privilege that women have erected.

By protesting that femininity is in one sense a series of artifices, the CD hopes to mitigate the prohibition against men dressing or acting like women. After all, since things such as cosmetics, pantyhose, and skirts have only an aesthetic, rather than a necessary, relationship to women, why can't men use them?

Men *can* indeed use them, so doesn't male usage render such items unisex? Not exactly. You see, the majority of men have no desire to either wear women's clothing or employ the other artifices of femininity. Are we then talking about a special class of men? Yes and no.

The CD's demand that he be allowed to freely appropriate the artifices and symbols of femininity is identical to the feminist demand that men share with women all of the prerogatives and symbols of masculinity.

An appropriate analogy is that of the Citadel. Not *all* women would care to attend this institute, whose unofficial credo, "2.0 and Go," should alert any intelligent candidate to look for a better school. However, the feminist protest surrounding the institute's refusal to admit Shannon Faulkner sought to establish the principle that *any woman who wishes to attend* should be free to do so. Likewise, not *all* men wish to act and dress like women, but *any man who wishes to do so* should have the right.

While Shannon Faulkner eventually resigned from the Citadel due to stress, she nevertheless made a gallant effort in challenging the strident sexism of that institution. And whereas the Citadel will undoubtedly remain populated mostly by men, there will certainly be female students in its future. Conversely, while femininity will remain predominantly the province of women, there will always be a few men who will want to be included.

Women have overwhelmingly repudiated gender roles in the past thirty years. Their message is that they don't want their sex to equate to a gender role. Some men echoed this sentiment beginning in the late seventies by demanding that their sex not equate to a fixed gender role either. One theme of male liberation—the acknowledgment of male sensitivity—highlighted yet another gender wrong that needed to be righted.

The old cultural formula that one's sex equates to a fixed gender role—as in Freud's dictum that anatomy is destiny—is clearly obsolete. The dictum, while true in its time, is now a non sequitur, for it doesn't logically follow that a penis or a vagina should predetermine a role in life. No person, man or woman, should have to live a life based upon a roll of the dice that took place at conception. CDs go a step further by arguing that they need not go through life wearing only the clothing that was assigned them based on this same role of dice.

TRANSGENDERISM AND THE QUESTION OF SEX-VERSUS-GENDER

The term *transgenderist* was coined by Virginia Prince to describe a person who lives in the gender role appropriate to the opposite sex. Prince's term was later appropriated by others and its meaning expanded. The term *transgenderism* now denotes a movement whose primary aim is to expand society's understanding of the differences between sex and gender. This distinction between sex and gender was first articulated by Dr. John Money in the 1950s.

Transgenderism, like feminism, argues that gender, or what we often call masculinity and femininity, has no logical or necessary connection to one's biological sex. Therefore, men and women should be free to cross over between masculinity and femininity as they please.

This approach seems reasonable enough until one notes that male transgenderists take an intellectual leap by using the sex-gender argument to justify calling themselves women. Upon what basis can TGs call themselves women? Certainly they're not referring to the biological, for breast implants and sexual reassignment surgery do not a woman make. While transsexualism is the closest that a man can come to being a woman, it's obviously not the same as being born a woman.

Some TGs who claim to be women are alluding to the fact that they assume the role of the woman during sex with men by being the receptor in oral and anal sex. By such logic any gay man who took the receptive role in sex would be considered a woman. This is absurd, for being the receptor in oral or anal sex no more makes one a woman than flying in an airplane makes one a bird.

A TG who calls himself a woman may be referring to his identification with cultural norms that we've come, rightly or wrongly, to identify with women. Does such identification make him a woman? Only if one believes that cultural norms define women.

In certain cultures there are men who choose to identify with the women of the tribe. In some Native American tribes, the *berdache* is a woman by virtue of his identification with, and compliance to, the feminine norms of the tribe. Some berdaches are holy men, others are simply men who do not choose to follow the path of the warrior. In such cultures it is not considered a disgrace for a man to choose the path of the berdache. A berdache, however, is expected to surrender the status accorded to the men of the tribe and assume the duties assigned to the women.

In our culture we do not have a precedent whereby a man can honorably identify with and adopt the way of the woman. Even if we did, the "way of the woman" would be considered sexist and artificial. We are not a small, isolated tribe with fixed gender roles. On the contrary, we represent many diverse tribes, or communities, with sometimes contradictory gender roles.

It is virtually impossible to arrive at a single, overriding definition of what a woman is. Considering the ideological distance between the definitions of Phyllis Schlafly and Gloria Steinem, one can easily see that a single definition of a woman would never suffice. Add to this the attempt to find a definition of woman that would include male-to-female transsexuals, and a semantic battleground is created.

Kate Bornstein, a post-op TS, has said of this matter:

> At this writing, some transgender activists are targeting lesbian separatists because the women have established something called "women-only spaces"; and a small number of these women will not brook the admission of transgendered women, whom the separatists don't see as women. . . .
>
> The current phraseology is "women born women." We're told that only "women born women" are allowed into some space. Well, that's a problem. Aside from the obvious absurdity of a newborn infant being called a woman, the phrase "woman born woman" just throws us back into the what's-a-woman question.

Bornstein sets up a bit of a smokescreen here. While it would obviously be absurd to call a newborn female a woman, we do call her a baby girl, girl being the juvenile version of a woman. Unfortunately we cannot escape the "what's-a-woman" question, for the struggle between "transgendered women" and "women born women" that Bornstein mentions is the crux of the problem we're addressing in this chapter.

Kate Millett made this assertion about the difference between male and female in her 1969 classic, *Sexual Politics:*

> Because of our social circumstances, male and female are really two cultures and their life experiences are utterly different—and this is crucial. Implicit in all the gender identity development which takes place through childhood is the sum total of the parents', the peers', and the culture's notion of what is appropriate to each gender by way of temperament, character, interests, status, worth, gesture, and expression. Every moment of the child's life is a clue to how he or she must think and behave to attain or satisfy the demands which gender places upon one.

Millett's observation is vital, for in so many ways males and females do live in separate cultures that are defined by biology, life experience, and gender. If there is a border between male and female that is not acknowledged by transgenderism, it is that of the life experience boundary cited by Millet. While I believe that the boundaries of *gender* should come down, the *life experience* boundary between male and female is one that needs to be recognized and affirmed.

In this vein, transgenderism's inexpert use of the sex/gender distinction has been criticized by John Money. In *Gay, Straight, and In-Between,* Money stated explicitly what he means by the sex/gender distinction:

> Although they are used carelessly and synonymously, sex and gender are not synonymous. They are also not antonyms, although they are frequently used almost as if they were. In one such usage, sex is defined as what you are born with, as male or female, and gender is what you acquire as a social role, from a social script. . . .
>
> In the years of childhood the gender-coded development of boys and girls invariably mirrors the masculine and feminine stereotypes of their social heritage. In the human species, there is no way in which to ascertain what culture-free masculinity and femininity would be like,

for they are always packaged in culture, just as linguistic ability is always packaged in a native language.

Gender, like language, permeates biology when it becomes encoded in the brain. It thus infuses learning, perception, and identity. At such a level of infusion, gender is transformed from being a set of mere social constructs to being a determinant in life experience.

Because transgenderism considers gender to be only a cultural matter, it defines "woman" as ultimately a constructed condition. I consider this definitional aspect of transgenderism to be its greatest weakness. If we diagram the sex/gender distinction of transgenderism, it looks like this:

Biological		Genderal
Female	Woman	Femininity
Male	Man	Masculinity

The words *man* and *woman* are not addressed in transgenderist theory per se; rather they are ideologically subsumed into *gender*. The problem is one of throwing out the baby with the bath water, for in the quest to find freedom of gender expression, transgenderism has reduced the state of *woman* to something that can be attained by surgery, hormones, or by merely distinguishing sex from gender. To summarily broker the life experience of women in such ways naturally draws the fire of "women born women."

The challenge in finding gender freedom lies in skillfully delinking *gender* from *life experience* rather than simply dissociating sex from gender. To my mind, the status of women definitionally fits between the sharp division of sex and gender that transgenderism insists upon. I believe that "man" and "woman" are experiential, or life-experience, conditions which arise from the confluence of the biological and the genderal. The transgenderal diagram should be modified as follows:

Biological	Experiential	Genderal
Female	Woman	Femininity
Male	Man	Masculinity

Transgenderism's strength is that it, like feminism, exposes the artificiality of gender roles and demands relief from such roles. Its weakness, like that of feminism, is that it often ignores or minimizes the experiential aspect of being a member of the opposite sex.

As Millet observed, ". . . male and female life experiences are utterly different—and this is crucial." To the extent that the TG calls himself a woman, he claims to experientially know what it is like to be a woman. Yet there is no way a TG could possibly obtain such knowledge.

If anything, the TG's experiential knowledge reflects the struggle of a man who has sought to incarnate his ideal of the woman he has always felt himself to be. It is only when the TG begins to pass unnoticed as a woman in society that (s)he can be said to appreciate somewhat the difficulties of being a woman as it relates to culture.

Further, a case could be made that the term *experiential*, as I have been using it, could be replaced with the word *ontological*, ontology being the branch of metaphysics which deals with the ultimate nature of being. What is it to be a woman? I don't know. I do believe, however, that the state of *woman* denotes a unique ontological status that a man can appreciate but never fully apprehend. And the opposite is true of men, for a woman can never finally understand what it is to be a man.

Yet feminist thought contains an error comparable to that of transgenderist thought. Rather than claiming to know what it's like to be a man, some feminists have instead invalidated the life experience and character of men, deeming them brutish, selfish, sexual predators whose punishment should be the immediate and unconditional surrender of their rights, income, and status.

Rather than sticking to the original premise that gender roles were flawed and that men had significant responsibility in the matter, some feminists instead launched a preemptive, wholesale attack upon men and male sexuality. Men have since dug in against feminism because they feel that the ongoing attack against them is unprincipled, generalized, and malicious—which in many cases it is.

SHOULD WE ABOLISH MALE AND FEMALE?

Transgender theory as articulated by Martine Rothblatt, whom I cited previously in chapter 4, takes a different approach to this matter of what a woman is than I do. While I advocate a sex/life experience/gender approach to looking at the issues of defining men and women, Rothblatt proposes a more radical approach. In her thinking, as presented in *The Apartheid of Sex,* the entire problem with sex and gender is rooted in the very concept of *male* and *female:*

The old gender paradigm is known as "sexual dimorphism" which means sex takes only two ("di") forms ("morphism"), male or female. It claims that this absolute division arises from sex-differentiated levels of hormones released prenatally, which in turn create not only two different reproductive systems, but also two different mental natures. From its ancient genesis, the old gender paradigm has been used to enforce the superiority of one apparent sex over the other and as a framework for research to prove one sex has a different nature from the other.

The new gender paradigm is called "sexual continuism." It posits that humanity is composed of a continuous blend of sexual identity, far beyond any simplistic male or female categorization. The new paradigm predicts that sexual identity, like other aspects of personality, arises from a confluence of factors not solely hormonal or environmental in origin. The new paradigm claims that reproductive systems are not strictly personal, but are sociotechnical and are accessible by all persons regardless of genitalia.

Rothblatt's thinking is reflected in *The International Bill of Gender Rights.* Adopted by the Second International Conference on Transgender Law and Employment Policy in 1993, this document asserts that

All human beings carry within themselves an ever unfolding idea of who they are and what they are capable of achieving. The individual's sense of self is not determined by chromosomal sex, genitalia, assigned birth sex, or initial gender role. Thus the individual's identity and capabilities cannot be circumscribed by what society deems to be masculine or feminine behavior. It is fundamental that individuals have the right to define, and to redefine as their lives unfold, their own gender identity, without regard to chromosomal sex, genitalia, assigned sex, or initial gender role.

Contemporary transgenderism embodies a sweeping vision of humanity in which all persons should be utterly free of any sexual or genderal definitions. How viable is such a vision? Could we indeed have a society in which *male* and *female* are obsolete terms?

To argue that we should negate the distinction between male and female because "humanity is composed of a continuous blend of sexual identity, far beyond any simplistic male or female categorization," presupposes that there is indeed a continuum within the matter of sex. Yet a continuum is defined as "a continuous whole, quantity, or series; a thing whose parts cannot be separated or separately discerned." The term *continuum* does not describe sex, for male and female do not form a seamless continuum. They instead comprise the two poles of biological reproduction.

That we distinguish male from female doesn't denote a gender paradigm; rather it indicates an evolutionary reality. Evolution has divided the human population roughly into equal numbers of males and females so that the species can be perpetuated and the gene pool continuously shuffled to ensure a healthier species.

Moreover, is humanity indeed "composed of a continuous blend of sexual identity"? The vast majority of the human population, or what we could call the *male/female mainstream,* is not in widespread revolt against the classifications of male and female. Further, the majority of the population is also heterosexual, and what is heterosexuality but a sexual attraction toward the opposite sex? Male and female are inescapable biological and sexual referents. To expect the mainstream to radically reinterpret itself for the sake of transgenderist ideology is the sort of conceit typical of a member of any minority.

I believe that there is no corrupt gender paradigm at work in the world. Rather, there's an evolutionary and sexual reality on top of which we have superimposed a set of dubious gender constructs. I assert that it is masculinity and femininity (gender), rather than male and female (sex), that form a continuum and therefore need redefinition.

Rothblatt seeks to bolster her argument that the distinction between male and female should be voided because reproductive systems are "not strictly personal, but are sociotechnical and accessible by all regardless of genitalia." While this certainly raises ethical issues of a medical and social nature, it is quite a leap to use such things as in vitro fertilization to justify abrogating the classifications of sex. That technology can aid reproduction hardly makes a case that the basis of reproduction—male and female—is obsolete.

The fact is that the majority of humanity doesn't suffer from the brain/body dissonance of transsexualism and so doesn't require redefinition. Revealingly, this brain/body dissonance is the basis upon which some transsexuals have claimed a type of psychological disability in order to compel private insurance companies and government agencies to pay for their reassignment surgery. That some transsexuals would claim a disability in order to receive medical benefits, while others insist that biology be redefined so that the taint of disability disappears ideologically, leaves me confused. Does transsexualism involve an actual disability or is it an issue that can be obviated by semantics?

It seems to me that the issue with a male-to-female TS calling himself a woman is ultimately concerned with the question of how we define reality. In the environment of political correctness, one's self-declaration is generally accepted in lieu of objective reality. Thus, when a male-to-female TS, for example, calls himself a woman, it is usually accepted without challenge.

Fearful of offending another, there is seldom debate about the truth or validity of such statements. This is particularly true when a person declares himself to be a victim. In the case of sexual continuism, the TS claims to be a victim of a torturous gender paradigm. However, such victimhood can exist only if we hold that male and female comprise an ideology rather than an evolutionary and biological reality.

That the male-to-female TS must undergo sexual reassignment surgery to find happiness indicates that his underlying distress is not due to a mere paradigm—otherwise he could just think differently to be happy. That he must undergo sexual reassignment surgery, that he must make his male genitals disappear, demonstrates that male and female, and thus sexual identity, are factual and discontinuous. The male-to-female transsexual is thus reacting to his inescapable, biological identity as a male when he goes under the knife.

There are three challenges in criticizing gender or the opposite sex. First, one cannot trivialize the unique life experience of the opposite sex by claiming to have an identical experience; this is the error of transgenderism. Second, it is wrong to turn the criticism of gender into an outright attack upon the opposite sex; this is the error of feminism. Finally, the attempt to negate the biological foundation of the race to achieve ideological hegemony is overreaching. Redefining culture, rather than biology, is the real challenge.

ANDROGYNY OR ASEXUALITY?

The demand that men be allowed to participate in femininity—and women in masculinity—raises yet another interesting question: If we blur masculinity and femininity, what will be left? How will we ultimately define gender? If men and women are to be truly equal, should masculinity and femininity merge into one androgynous, indivisible form of gender, or should we seek to remove the sexual connotation from gender altogether?

SHOULD GENDER BE ANDROGYNOUS?

At first the idea of merging masculinity and femininity in order to create an androgynous society recalls the bland, androgynous Chinese society of Maozedong. Of course in America a society of androgynes would likely be carried to bizarre and entertaining heights—much as one already sees at Club Fuck and other underground clubs in Los Angeles and New York. Nevertheless, the notion of an androgynous society misses the whole point of cross-dressing.

CDs would abhor an androgynous society because it would destroy the very thing they seek: the experience of being womanlike. Androgyny allows for a person to exhibit characteristics of both masculinity and femininity. When the CD cross-dresses, however, he is only interested in imitating a woman. The contrast between masculinity and femininity is therefore critical to the cross-dressing experience.

My argument that masculinity and femininity should be understood as mere gender constructs is not an attempt to destroy or negate the two. I contend instead that we must redefine masculinity and femininity as forms of personal expression that should be available to either sex. By recognizing gender as a matter of personal expression, males and females can be freed from the tyranny of enforced compliance with the prevailing cultural dictates of gender.

By shifting the focus of gender in this manner, masculinity and femininity can be recast as distinctive styles which are aesthetically attractive and enjoyable. Ultimately human freedom demands that males and females should be allowed to be as masculine or feminine as they please. My argument, then, is not for androgyny, but rather for a freedom of gender expression that is independent of one's born sex.

SHOULD GENDER BE ASEXUAL?

What about asexuality? Does our call for freedom of expression render masculinity and femininity asexual? Asexuality means "that which has no sexual nature." In legal matters, we already strive for asexuality, or what we call *equality*, between men and women. The law allows for no distinction between the sexes to be made. After all, no one should be harassed or discriminated against because of his or her sex.

But gender is not treated asexually; society infuses it with sexuality. At the same time it legislates against discrimination based on sex, it ostracizes feminine men and masculine women. Society still mandates that males should be masculine and females should be feminine. Is it possible to treat gender asexually?

Do you think you could view a cross-dresser asexually? Do you think you could see a man dressed as a woman and *not* assign a sexual meaning to his cross-dressing? The CD presents us with the need to distinguish between sexuality and gender. We already do so when we assign no sexual significance the wearing of men's clothes by women. Indeed, virtually every item that was once considered menswear has become an acceptable part of every woman's wardrobe. So why shouldn't the reverse be true?

When a woman wears men's clothing she partakes of the masculine without seeking to destroy it, and she retains her womanhood. No aspersion is cast on her for wearing clothing worn by the opposite sex. It is both logical and egalitarian to suggest that men should enjoy the same prerogative, namely, they should be able to partake freely of the feminine without any sexual, and by implication pathological, meaning.

GENDER HYPOCHONDRIA

Just as you have suspected, the concept of gender is fairly beaten to death in the TG community. It gets so much scrutiny and blame because transgenderists are extremely sensitive to afflictions of gender. The medical term for a disease of gender is *genderitis*. Everyone suffers from genderitis periodically—particularly when he or she has to perform some loathsome task that isn't required of the opposite sex.

I have identified a syndrome I call *gender hypochondria* to denote the chronic, and often imaginary, anxiety that some TGs exhibit about the state of their gender. They claim that their very bad case of genderitis is the cause of all of their woes. "If society/my parents/my wife/my employer would only realize that I need to live and dress like a woman all of the time, then my health, mood, and finances would improve," goes the litany.

Is there a cure for genderitis? Not at present, but medical science is busy studying its causes and possible cures. If enough interest is generated in the malady, then perhaps we will be able to have our first genderitis telethon next summer.

THE CD AND HIS WIFE

The ultimate arena in which *man* and *woman* and *masculinity* and *femininity* are defined is in intimate relations between the two. In this section I want to focus on the gender issues that come up in the relations between the heterosexual CD and his wife.

To be a CD is to be a member of a minority, and no one completely understands the intensity with which a minority member feels the tooth of prejudice except another member of that minority. Minorities may seem to overreact to prejudice; they may seem hypersensitive. However, if one has never walked the proverbial mile in another's moccasins, how can he fully appreciate his fellow's plight?

A CD faces a highly personal struggle with the gender issues we've discussed—particularly with his wife or girlfriend. The cultural implications of gender are hammered home with great force when a CD becomes romantically involved with a woman. A woman who loves a CD cannot be objectively detached from his cross-dressing, nor can she be expected to always be enlightened or accepting. She may well not want the world to know that her husband enjoys dressing like a woman. Even if she intellectually accepts that the constructs of femininity are baseless, she may still be uneasy about her husband or boyfriend trafficking in them.

Although he might speak in an enlightened and passionate way about the injustice of culture and its gender expectations, if a CD's wife or girlfriend doesn't care to see him dressed like a woman, then his cross-dressing will either have to be done outside of the relationship or it will become a source of conflict.

When a woman is emotionally involved with a CD, the idea of trespassing arises. For example, if we were to ask the wife or girlfriend of a CD what her predominant feelings about cross-dressing were, we would probably find that what she resented most was her husband's intrusion into her sacred realm. In my experience, many such women feel that their CD husband or boyfriend is somehow "competing" with them for femininity.

"How would you like it if I didn't shave my legs, strapped on a dildo, and wore BVDs to bed?" was a question I was once asked by a woman whom I dated for a very short time. I told her that I understood her resentment, and then I asked her if I should feel the same sort of resentment about a female boss. She glared at me and said no, that it would be sexist for a man to feel resentment in reporting to a female manager.

She thought it was acceptable for me to work for a woman, but not for me to dress like a woman (although dressing like the boss is the first rule of success!). I then asked her if my cross-dressing would make any difference to her if we weren't dating. She admitted that it wouldn't.

I think her response sums up the general attitude of most women toward cross-dressing: I don't mind it as long as the man I'm with doesn't do it. Tip O'Neill's maxim that "politics is always local" is analogous in that gender issues are always personal. Most people don't really care about any issue unless it affects them directly—and so it is with the CD and gender.

The heterosexual CD will be hard-pressed to enjoy the freedom of gender expression unless the woman in his life can accept his cross-dressing. Wouldn't it just be easier if the CD never married? Yes, but most heterosexual CDs prefer the intimacy of a relationship to bachelorhood in skirts.

Cross-dressing, while pleasurable, is seldom fulfilling enough for most men to build an entire life upon, for it lacks the emotional contentment that only another person can give. Thus, the CD hopes to find a woman who can understand and accept his need for the feminine. This is not an easy task, particularly to the degree that a woman insists that her man fit the cultural requirements of masculinity.

If a woman is accepting of her partner's cross-dressing, then his self-expression can unfold. If she's not accepting, but there is still enough love between them to sustain a relationship, then they must find a compromise. In the absence of compromise—and the commitment to the relationship that it declares—the CD is left to express his gender preferences outside of the relationship with his wife. Unfortunately this is the route that most married CDs are forced to take, for it remains understandably difficult for a wife to see her husband dressed like a woman.

Many CDs get married with the thought that marriage will somehow cure their cross-dressing; their wives also marry them with this same hope. But this doesn't happen. Thus, comments such as "My husband would be perfect if he weren't a cross-dresser" become common among the wives of CDs. Denial, resentment, and secrecy inevitably become part of such marriages.

The best advice I can give is for couples to seek counseling on the issues of cross-dressing and gender prior to marriage. Most women can live with a guy who golfs or bowls too much, but few can live with a guy who likes to wear her clothes. And even fewer can accept and remain committed to a man who wants to become a woman.

TODAY ON TABLOID TALK: CROSS-DRESSERS AND THE MEN WHO HATE THEM

Women are not the only ones who find objectionable the idea of a man trying to become a woman: Some men also find the idea offensive. To my great benefit, my male friends have always accepted with humor and grace the fact that I'm a CD. On those occasions when I've been out in public cross-dressed, most men who read me as a CD seemed indifferent. A few, however, have been openly hostile.

One time I went dressed as a woman to a Halloween party at a nightclub. I was with several friends, so I felt safe. At one point in the evening I had to use the restroom. Although I normally use the women's restroom when I'm out cross-dressed in public, this was Halloween and I felt that I was too conspicuous: I was dressed like a French maid. I decided I had better use the men's room lest I be asked to leave the club.

In the men's room a short, squat, drunken fellow accosted me. He said that I was a "disgusting faggot who ought to be shot." I ignored him. I began to dry my hands when he suddenly took a swing at me. I deflected the blow and forcefully shoved my open palm against his forehead, driving his porcine head hard against the tiled wall.

He hadn't been expecting my reaction. It quickly occurred to him that under the dress was a man who was bigger, stronger, and more sober than he. Undoubtedly the last thing he wanted was to have his ass kicked by a pissed-off queen in the men's room: How would he explain that to his friends? After a tense moment he edged along the wall and headed out the door.

Why did this guy hate me so? Because he had been raised to despise effeminacy in himself and other men. Male gender roles can be brutish. For this reason I advocate that the CD tell very few people about his interests. Until one is sure that another man is tolerant and open-minded, why invite trouble?

The cross-dresser poses a problem for certain other men because he breaks rules. He is a man who dresses and acts like a woman, breaking one of the strongest rules about masculinity in our male-dominant culture—namely that men do not dress or act like women.

This rule, however, reveals an enormous prejudice toward women. After all, what is wrong with a man dressing or acting like a woman? Nothing, unless you believe that being male is far superior to being female, and that for a man to stoop to the level of being a woman is degrading.

In our male metaculture women are still assigned lower status. It remains beneath most men's dignity to be thought of as a woman, because womanliness in men culturally suggests lack of aggression, indecision, and other disabilities men falsely assign to women. But worse yet, no man wants to be thought of in womanly terms because it implies weakness, and weakness falsely denotes homosexuality.

Professionally I'm a salesperson for a large corporation. One day I called on one of my profane, hotheaded male customers and was confronted with a diatribe that amazed even a polluted, worldly salesman such as myself. The following represents an extreme example, but in illustrating the worst elements of male culture it is nonetheless instructive. The conversation went something like this:

CUSTOMER: I just saw your competitor, and I'm about ready to throw him out of here!

ME: Why?

CUSTOMER: He tried to screw me on some prices! (Getting angrier) I guess he thought I was just some goddamn woman! That guy just wanted to fuck me in the ass! I might as well have laid down and let that guy fuck me right in the ass like I was some goddamn woman!

ME: (Expressing my sarcasm) You know, you don't have to be a woman to get fucked in the ass.

CUSTOMER: (Laughing, not getting the point) Well, I guess not if you're a goddamn queer!

I work in a professional environment, but sometimes the truth erupts from under the social veneer. Besides pointing out what one has to occasionally put up with in sales, this story shows the extreme contempt that some men have for women and gays (and how seriously many customers regard the issue of price!). To them, "getting fucked in the ass" is an act that demonstrates submission and endorses male power and contempt for women. To the extent that a homosexual would get "fucked in the ass," he is no better than a woman.

Historically, some armies sodomized male prisoners and raped female captives. Why? The male victors wanted to humiliate the male prisoners by degrading their manhood, and they felt that raping the women was a just reward for conquest. Sexual debasement as the prerogative of the conqueror is an ancient notion that still influences the male psyche: Women are there to fuck, and if another man gets in your way, then a real man ought to "fuck him in the ass" by ruining him in a literal or figurative way.

The notion of the all-conquering penis as a tool of power and vengeance still resonates. To the extent that this notion implies that women are inferior, it reinforces the idea that a real man would never lower himself to acting or dressing like a woman. Similarly the notion that a real man should beat up and degrade any male who dares challenge his masculinity also reinforces the idea that if a man is not a real man, he's a wimp, or a woman.

To parody the severity with which males are judged for saying or doing anything feminine, I wrote the following "TV Social Register" column. What was disturbing was that some of my readers thought that I was reporting on an actual event. One PPOC member even called to confess that he had this very problem.

———————————

ALARMING NEW BEHAVIOR IDENTIFIED IN MALES
A Shocking Report of Deviance
by Justine Sahnjay, Health and Beauty Editor

Sex researcher Dr. George Dukasis of the University of Cincinnati has identified an alarming new behavior in some males. "It seems that certain men have a perverse need to use women's hygiene products," Dr. Dukasis noted.

The syndrome was first discovered when Fred S., a 28-year-old machinist from Duluth, saw the doctor last year for treatment of a compulsion to use his wife's "floral scented" underarm deodorant and other products.

"I can't help myself," Fred S. lamented. "It began when I was a boy. I innocently used my mother's Avon Gentle Lavender shampoo. I found I liked it much more than the harsh Head and Shoulders I had been using."

Soon, Fred S. found himself caught in a web of deceit as he sneaked his mother's hygiene products. "I did it all," Fred S. confessed, "Lady Speed Stick, L'Oreal Hair Conditioner for Women, Correctol—the Ladies' Gentle Laxative, and even Pamprin for headaches."

Fred thought that he would be able to quit this odd habit when he married, but it only became worse. "I knew I had hit bottom," he confided, "when my wife caught me using her Summer's Eve douche. I know it sounds strange, but some days I just had, you know, that 'not so fresh feeling,' and I liked the mountain meadow smell." To stave off a divorce, Fred S. agreed to seek treatment.

When news of this case first hit the airwaves, Dr. Dukasis was inundated with calls from loved ones, victims, and the actual sufferers of this aberration he terms *transhygienism,* which is the desire to use the hygiene products of the opposite sex. "While transhygienism occurs predominantly in men," Dr. Dukasis remarked, "I do have an unusual case of an elderly woman who uses Cruex."

The doctor's chief mode of treatment has been aversion therapy. "I hook electrodes up to the patient's genitals and have them apply the hygiene products of the opposite sex. At random intervals I deliver 5,000-volt surges. Soon the patient is too disoriented and too afraid to indulge in his inordinate and unnatural behavior.

"The real danger to society," the doctor warned, "is that this compulsion may progress from hygiene products to, dare I say, cosmetics!" In a shocking scenario, the doctor even predicted that a transhygienist could, like many a drug user, escalate his "habit" from a seemingly "innocent shampoo" to a full-blown case of cross-dressing!

"God forbid that this should ever happen," Dr. Dukasis solemnly intoned, comparing such behavior to those that took place in the decadent last days of the Roman Empire. A government panel has been formed to study the problem.

Masculinity and femininity cannot be put into either a neat cultural formula or a bottle of shampoo. Until we tear down the boundaries that keep people from attaining the freedom to express themselves as they please, we will continue to suffer everything from the trivial absurdities of such things as "the ladies' gentle laxative" to the significant tyrannies of sexism and gender discrimination. The man in the red velvet dress, for his part, stands on the boundary between masculinity and femininity to remind us all that there is often no more than window dressing between the two worlds.

7

THE BLACK LACE PRISON

C ross-dressing, like shooting whitewater rapids, is full of excitement and risk. When a man cross-dresses he goes beyond the safety of the charted waters of masculinity and enters the roiling waters on the edge of his psyche. Most men come through the experience with an expanded sense of self that encompasses masculinity and femininity; other men crash onto the rocks and ruin their lives.

While most cross-dressing behavior is innocent, albeit unusual, for some it is tied into larger personality disorders. In this chapter we'll meet two CDs who exhibit maladaptive behavior. Though they represent a minority within the world of cross-dressing, their behavior is more sensational and so naturally receives much greater attention and interest than does that of the quiet, everyday CD. It will become evident in the course of our review that for this minority, cross-dressing is part and parcel of a highly unhealthy personality and lifestyle.

Cross-dressing is not entirely harmless; it carries with it certain psychological risks, two of the biggest being guilt and narcissistic self-absorption. Guilt arises because many men feel that this behavior is wrong, yet they enjoy it and continue to do it. Narcissistic self-absorption occurs because cross-dressing can be so intensely pleasurable that it becomes a world unto itself, and all the CD cares to think about are the pleasures and problems of his own cross-dressed personage.

The *Black Lace Prison* is the term I use to describe the hell that maladaptive cross-dressing can become for both the CD and those close to him. I think this term conveys the agonizing duality of eroticism and guilt that many a troubled CD feels. On the one hand, the sensuality and sexual pleasure that the CD derives from indulging his feminine persona and wearing women's clothing is intense. On the other hand, the CD often feels guilty because his behavior typically takes place in secret, and he might also engage in behaviors which can cause him a great deal of harm.

Compounding all of this is the CD's knowledge that he can no more stop cross-dressing than a river can flow backward. The CD thus faces a simple but brutal choice: either accept his behavior and work to integrate it into his life in a healthy fashion, or continue to indulge his guilty pleasures and let them metamorphose into a self-destructive drama.

To integrate such a difficult behavior requires that one admit the truth: I am a cross-dresser. Based upon this admission, one can then begin to communicate with others about it. Communication can take the form of therapy, premarital or marital counseling, joining a support group, or simply talking to a trusted friend or family member. This done, one must also begin to voluntarily control his conduct, to seek balance, and to negotiate the practical matters of time and money.

The value of therapy, in particular, is that it can help the CD to sort things out. Cross-dressing can be a polarizing behavior, causing such stigma that it is blamed for all of the CD's problems. A useful insight I had in the course of therapy was the realization that most of my problems exist independently of my cross-dressing. Even if I could take a magic pill and make cross-dressing disappear from my life, most of my psychological and situational difficulties would still exist.

There's always hope for a person who feels pain, who knows that he needs help. But a person who is oblivious to his problems can only become stranger still, and this is particularly true in the case of dysfunctional transvestites. You will meet few people weirder than some of the hyperneurotic CDs running loose out there. Such people often prove to be reckless time bombs, startlingly pathetic losers, or both.

To illustrate my assertion, imagine that your strangest male relative, in addition to his other neuroses, has a compulsive need to wear dresses. Such a person would very probably be considered weird on a super-tanker-size scale. This is because peculiar behavior of a sexual nature—as cross-dressing is often perceived to be—is always more noticeable than its underlying motivation.

A frequent temptation is to simply dismiss such people as sexual perverts. But what is a sexual perversion? Traditional psychoanalytic thinking deemed sexual perversion to be any deviation from the norm. In their 1973 book, *The Language of Psychoanalysis,* Laplanche and Pontalis defined sexual perversion in this way:

> Deviation from the "normal" sexual act when this is defined as coitus with a person of the opposite sex directed towards the achievement of orgasm by means of genital penetration.
>
> Perversion is said to be present: where the orgasm is reached with other sexual objects (homosexuality, paedophilia, bestiality, etc.) or through other regions of the body (anal coitus, etc.); where the orgasm is subordinated absolutely to certain extrinsic conditions, which may even be sufficient in themselves to bring about sexual pleasure (fetishism, transvestism, exhibitionism, and sadomasochism).
>
> In a more comprehensive sense, "perversion" connotes the whole of the psychosexual behavior that accompanies such atypical means of attaining sexual pleasure.

This sweeping definition amounts to an almost wholesale condemnation of any sexual expression except heterosexual intercourse.

A more contemporary clinical definition states that sexual perversion is the *habitual and obligatory restriction of sexual fantasy and behavior.* What does this mean? Sexual fantasy or behavior can be habitual without being perverted, as is, for example, sex within marriage. The *obligatory restriction* of sexual fantasy or behavior, however, refers to a condition in which a person has little or no choice over a given sexual script, for he is restricted to fantasizing and behaving in a particular way.

Yet what is heterosexuality except the habitual and obligatory restriction of sexual fantasy and behavior? The female heterosexual, for example, restricts her sexuality to men, and even then she is usually obligated to have sex only with her husband. The heterosexual female also fantasizes exclusively about men, for lesbianism holds no attraction for her. That heterosexuality can, absurdly, be made to fit the prevailing definition of sexual perversion calls attention to the difficulty of trying to define sexual perversion.

The concept of sexual perversion assumes that one knows what "normal" is. But even heterosexual monogamy within marriage, long considered to be the benchmark of normalcy, can be riddled with problems. Spousal abuse, impotence, adultery, abortion, and divorce argue for the fact that marriages, just like individuals, can be judged only on a case-by-case basis.

Homosexual behavior, long considered to be the benchmark of deviance, was thought unquestionably in the past to be a sexual perversion. However, therapists now distinguish between healthy homosexual behavior and perverted homosexual behavior. The distinction is rooted in the acceptance of homosexuality as an alternative sexual orientation rather than as a de facto sexual perversion.

Thus, while there can be perverted behavior in *individual* homosexuals, not *all* homosexuals are perverted. The emphasis in therapy has become one of eliminating unhealthy behavior rather than changing sexual orientation. Using this distinction, it is possible to see that not all cross-dressing behavior is perverted—an important fact for the CD and those close to him to understand. Still, many behaviors such as cross-dressing or anal sex are considered deviant simply because they are deemed "immoral."

The religious right views sexuality solely in terms of "moral" and "immoral." But what if a free individual doesn't subscribe to biblical morality? The religious right responds by saying that the Bible offers moral absolutes, and, in the absence of such absolutes, there can be only moral relativism, moral anarchy, and societal breakdown. Based on the lofty notion of saving us all, the religious right asserts that any sexual behavior that is not biblically sanctioned fosters societal breakdown, or more particularly the destruction of family values (a euphemism for Judeo-Christian morality), and hence should be outlawed and made an object of shame.

Yet the standard by which to evaluate sexual behavior cannot be one of moral absolutes, because it demands that one version of morality should prevail, which in turn degenerates into religious and philosophical warfare. Rather, an important criterion should be to ask what rights to self-expression people have in a free society.

The Declaration of Independence and the Bible, as the religious right supposes, are not one and the same document. The Declaration of Independence states that men are endowed by their Creator with the unalienable right to life, liberty, and the pursuit of happiness. Given that sexual expression constitutes a pursuit of happiness, the question of sexual expression in a democracy can be spoken of only in terms of what is legal or illegal, our communal system of law rightly being the final arbiter of allowable sexual expression.

Religion and law aside, there exist well-established psychological criteria by which to determine if cross-dressing or other types of sexual behavior are problematic. When an individual CD is evaluated in light of these criteria, it quickly becomes apparent whether his cross-dressing is maladaptive or not. Let's briefly review and comment upon these criteria:

1. *Is the person in distress over his behavior?* A well-adjusted heterosexual has no reason to seek counseling or believe that his sexuality is perverted. A heterosexual who is in distress over the fact the he must peer into bedroom windows at night, however, obviously needs counseling. In the case of cross-dressing, the question would be whether the CD is in distress over his behavior. Does he feel guilty, obsessed, out of control, or ashamed? If so, he would benefit from therapy.

2. *Is the behavior causing major disruptions to family, work, or social relationships?* A woman who avoids her husband and children to carry on an adulterous affair significantly disrupts her family relationships. A man who uses his expense account or paycheck to pay for phone sex jeopardizes his job and marriage. A man who demands that his wife perform fellatio on him every day may cause her a great deal of misery. A CD who spends money he doesn't have on women's

clothing, stays out late, and lies to his wife about his activities is like-wise disrupting his family life.

3. *Does the behavior pose a threat to the person's health or the health of those around him?* While sexual practices such as bondage and discipline pose a risk of injury, other practices such as autoerotic asphyxiation place a person in extreme danger; over 1,000 deaths per year in the United States are attributed to this behavior.

Despite the risks, people continue to engage in dangerous sexual conduct, such as engaging in sex with prostitutes, that places them at risk of injury or contracting AIDS or other sexually transmitted diseases. The real tragedy of all of this is that the sexual dilettante not only places himself in peril, but he also exposes those around him to disease and the possibility of premature death.

4. *Does the behavior prevent the person from using his potential? Does it limit initiative, stifle self-growth, or inhibit creativity?* A person who consistently stays home to watch pornography and masturbate in lieu of doing something that may benefit him socially or intellectually, for example, is in need of counseling. Likewise, the person who avoids the pressures and challenges of life by retreating into cross-dressing or other forms of sexuality is clearly using sex as an avoidance mechanism.

5. *Does the behavior require the person to engage in illegal activities?* Whether such things as pornography and prostitution constitute actual crimes can be debated. The problems with these two activities, at least in my mind, are more properly those of money, time, adultery, and risk of disease. Other sex crimes, however, particularly rape and child molestation, are indicative of a seriously disordered personality and require treatment.

These criteria can help to evaluate sexual behavior in a way that is ethical, humane, and intelligent. They also show that maladaptive sexual behavior transcends the simplistic division of homosexual and heterosexual. Sexual problems are human problems. People from every walk of life, racial origin, religion, and economic status are affected by sexual problems.

Cross-dressing is but one of the many forms of human sexual expression, and, as with any other form, there exist CDs with maladaptive behavior. How does such behavior manifest itself in a CD's life? I want to present the stories of two CDs who exhibit maladaptive sexual behavior. It will quickly become apparent in the first story that cross-dressing is the least of Yvonne's problems. In the second story, cross-dressing plays a significant role in Larry's life.

YVONNE'S STORY

After I got out of the Navy in 1985, I got my own apartment. It was there that I started to explore my long-suppressed desires to dress like a woman. I'd always wanted to try it, but I was afraid. The first time I completely cross-dressed, I had to get blotto just to get past the guilt.

I went to a dirty bookstore looking for information on cross-dressing. What I found instead were books about guys getting dressed up like women and getting it on with men. There were also other books about little fairy boys being forced to dress up in women's clothing by dominant women.

I was aware that I might have bisexual feelings, so the idea of being with a man interested me. But at the same time the thought scared me. I thought that if I had sex with a guy I would turn gay and never get married, and I wanted to get married. I decided that it would be best to stop at cross-dressing.

One day I was in the bookstore and this really good-looking transvestite came in to look at the books. After she left I asked the manager if it would be all right if I came into his store dressed like a woman. He said he liked to have TVs around because it was good for business. I was glad to hear this because I didn't have any places to go when I was dressed; I had been staying at home, and it had gotten boring.

The next time I got dressed I decided to go to the bookstore. I sat in my apartment before I left and had a few drinks to screw up my courage. I couldn't believe I was actually going to go into a public place dressed like a woman! I had on a blond wig, black leather skirt, yellow silk blouse, and black hose and heels. I was on cloud nine.

When I got there the manager gave me a lot of compliments. He told me that I ought to go check out the she-male videos in the twenty-five-cent booths. Getting ten bucks in quarters, I headed back to the booths and started watching the videos. I got super turned on! Here were these sexy she-males having hot sex in their lingerie. My heart was pounding. I actually started rubbing myself right in the booth. I knew that the guys in the other booths did, so I figured why not? I just sort of slid down my hose and panties and did it. It was a lot of fun because it was so nasty. I wound up buying two TV videos and taking them home.

I went back to the bookstore a couple of weeks later all dressed up so I could get some more videos. I had a terrific buzz on and felt like I was the sexiest thing in the world. I went into a booth to preview a few videos before I bought them. As I was watching, a guy came up and stood next to my booth. Without a word of introduction, he said, "I'm really into TVs and I think you're a fox!" I was flattered. After we exchanged pleasantries, he asked me if I wanted to go over to his place for a drink. I knew what he wanted and I was game. I followed him over to his house. I was nervous. I felt like a girl on my first date.

When we got to his place, he put on a TV video, poured me a drink, and we sat down on the couch and started talking. After a while I went to pour myself another drink. He got up, walked over to me, and put his arms around me. I was extremely aroused. As we started necking, he reached down and grabbed my ass. Before I knew it I was on my knees giving my first blow job. The experience confirmed my bisexuality. It was so exciting that I just quit dating women so that I could experiment with this part of my life.

I had been dating this guy for about two months when he announced that he didn't think he should see me anymore because his wife suspected that he was having an affair. It didn't matter because I had gotten some other numbers from guys I had met at the bookstore. Soon I was seeing three guys. Since I made them all wear condoms, I felt like I was being responsible. For a while it was all wonderful and new. I was having all of this great sex, living out all of the fantasies I'd seen on the videos—hell, I felt like a kid in a candy store.

About this time I discovered the Queen Mary. The Queen Mary is a nightclub in Los Angeles that features a female impersonation show. The show is always good, but the real action is in the back bar. Called the King's Den, the back bar is where CDs and the men who get off on them hang around. I met some new guys in there, and soon I had all the dates I wanted.

People don't realize it, but there are a lot of guys who are into CDs. Most of these guys are married and, if anything, they say that their wives aren't as feminine as the CDs they meet. I know that none of my girlfriends owned even a fraction of the nice lingerie I did. Hell, none of my girlfriends ever once wore a garter belt and stockings to bed.

In the King's Den I always felt just like a real woman in a regular bar. A guy would catch my eye, we'd talk, and then he'd buy me a drink. If we liked each other, the topic of sex would come up pretty quickly. I was into giving head; I really liked to give head when I was dressed up. Usually, if we hit it off we'd go over to the guy's motel room or his house.

I always liked to neck with a guy for a while and then get him naked. Then I would get up from the bed and slowly undress for him. Unzipping my dress, I would let it slide down to the floor. Underneath I'd wear a camisole and tap pants with stockings, or a full corset, but usually it was a bra and panties with a garter belt and stockings. I'm slender and I don't have much body hair, so I thought I looked sexy. The guy would usually start pumping his rod and beckon me over. I'd slide back onto the bed, slip a condom on him, and start doing him.

I never wanted a guy to go down on me because the thought of a man sucking my dick bothered me. Also, I never did anal sex. It just seemed too, and I know this sounds weird, but it just seemed too gay, and I'm not a homosexual. I don't have anything against them, but I'm just not one of them. Some of the guys I was with wanted to fuck me, so I would let them slide their dick between my closed legs while they laid on top of me.

Having all this sex made me wonder why I had waited so long to get in touch with my feminine and bisexual feelings. I really did feel like a woman when I was having sex with a man. I guess the reason why I didn't want my cock to play a role in sex was because it would shatter the illusion.

I went on living this life for about two years. Then one day at work I met Cindy, the woman who would become my wife. She seemed perfect. We started dating and really hit it off. When I told her about my cross-dressing it didn't seem to faze her. I didn't tell her about my bisexuality, though. I figured I would tell her later when the time was right. I quit having sex with guys because I started to feel guilty. Cindy made me feel wonderful and I felt like it just wasn't right to fool around on her.

Cindy got pregnant about six months after we met. I was glad because I'd always wanted kids. We went to Vegas and got married right away and she moved in with me when we got back. That's when things started going bad. Cindy wanted me to stop getting dressed so much. She also didn't like me buying dirty books or going to the bookstore. As a compromise, we agreed that I could go to the Queen Mary on Saturday nights.

Once my daughter was born I found that I was becoming bored with marriage and domestic life. I missed being able to go on dates with guys. My wife didn't have a very strong sex drive after the baby, but mine hadn't changed. I started to buy TV books and videos again. Cindy found some of them one day and was furious. She accused me of being gay, of not wanting to stay married, of wasting money on cross-dressing, and of lying. This episode started the ball rolling downhill.

With three months my marriage was going down the toilet. We were always fighting. Cindy was always complaining that she had to borrow money from her mother because I spent ours on cross-dressing. But that wasn't true; the fact was that my hours had been cut back at work.

The only reason we were staying together was because of the baby. I got so tired of the bullshit that I'd usually start a fight on Saturday morning so that I'd have an excuse to storm out of the

155 • THE BLACK LACE PRISON

house and not come back until late that night or the next morning. Once I got out of the house, I would head over to the mall to do some shopping for Yvonne. It usually didn't matter what I bought—a blouse, some high heels, a new lipstick—it just felt good to transition into my other self. After shopping, I'd have lunch and then go over to my buddy Stan's house.

Stan is a CD. He's divorced and so doesn't mind the company. Anyway, I'd start getting dressed around four o'clock. By seven Stan [Crystal] and I were ready to head out on the town. We'd usually start with dinner at one of the gay restaurants over in West Hollywood. After dinner we always went over to the Queen Mary.

One night, after a particularly vicious fight with Cindy, she did the proverbial thing where she took the baby and went home to mother. I got the papers a few weeks later and it looked like Cindy was absolutely going to nail my ass to the wall for child support. To add insult to injury, she called me to tell me that I needed help, that I was an alcoholic and a pervert. She also told me that she had a new boyfriend and not to come around to see my daughter without calling three days ahead of time.

I was so angry that the first thing I did was to call up one of my old boyfriends. We got together at his place and had one hell of a time. The sex helped me to relax. I found that I could keep my mind off Cindy and the divorce by dressing up, partying with other CDs, and going out with guys. About this time, I'd stopped using condoms because I discovered that I liked sex more without them. It's called "wet sex" and it's a whole lot better than sucking on latex. You just have to make sure that the person you're with isn't a sleaze.

One day Cindy came by unexpectedly to drop off some more legal papers. When the doorbell rang I thought it was one of my CD friends so I yelled "Come on in!" I was dressed up and one of my "dates" was sitting in the living room. We had been drinking and were somewhat disheveled. It was real obvious to Cindy what was going on. As she was leaving, just to be a prick, I said, "Look, I've got a new boyfriend, why don't you call three days in advance before you come over?"

That whole year after we split up I was nothing but a whore; I did one guy after another. I knew what I was doing hurt Cindy, but her having replaced me with another guy so fast hurt me a lot, so I guess I was trying to get even. Anyway, I'm sure she was having an affair with her boyfriend before we split up. I got so pissed off that I quit paying her child support. I figured that she could just sue me.

The turning point came for me one Friday night when I picked up this guy at the Queen Mary. He worked for the IRS and seemed to be a decent enough guy. After having a few drinks, we took his car over to a cheap motel nearby where he had gotten a room. We started necking. I undressed him and then went through my little striptease. He seemed a little more excited than most of the guys I'd been with; he was acting hyper and kind of wild. But what the hell, I figured, he was probably new to all of this and was nervous and excited like I used to get.

I climbed into the bed next to the guy and began to go down on him. Suddenly he pulled a pair of handcuffs from under the pillow and slipped one of the cuffs around my right wrist.

"What the hell are you doing!" I yelled at him.

"I want you to be my piss slave," he said.

"I'm not into that," I told him. I pulled away and quickly fastened the other cuff around my right wrist so that he couldn't handcuff both hands. I knew from one of my friends that there's an etiquette to bondage and discipline. If someone's into it, he's supposed to tell you first, and the then the two of you agree to the scenario that's going to be acted out. Also, you're supposed to have a code word to be used if it gets too heavy for the person being tied up. The fact that this guy didn't tell me what he was up to scared me.

"What kind of fuckin' prick-teaser are you?" he shouted as he grabbed me by the arms. He must have thought I was playing a game with him because then he laughed and said, "Daddy's little cocksucking bitch better finish sucking Daddy's big dick before she gets a good ass-whipping."

I stood up and told the guy that I was leaving, that I didn't want to finish. He got out of bed, grabbed his pants, and walked to the door in order to block me from leaving. Pulling the belt off his pants, he doubled it over and whipped the chair with it.

"You'd better be fuckin' kiddin'," he said, as he glared at me with a real freaky look in his eyes.

I'm not a big guy, but he was, and he was madder than hell. I could just see the headlines: Transvestite found dead in Sherman Oaks hotel room.

"Yeah, I was just screwing with you," I said nervously as I walked over to him and grabbed his dick. I kneeled down and finished the blow job, afraid to do anything else. Thank God he didn't try anything weird.

After he came, I stood up and turned around to get my dress. He lashed out unexpectedly with his belt and whipped me on the ass. I spun around and he kept whipping me. I covered my face and begged him to stop. He stopped whipping me and suddenly pulled the wig off my head and threw it down.

"You goddamn little cocksucking queer," he snarled. With that he pushed me to the floor, grabbed my panties, and pulled them off. "Look at that little dick of yours," he sneered. "No wonder you have to suck dicks, you could never get a woman with a dick like that!"

Oh my god, I thought, what the hell have I gotten myself into? He's some friggin' crazy pervert who's going to beat the hell out me or kill me. As I lay there frozen in fear, he laughed at me again.

"You're so fuckin' tense," he said. "Let me get something to loosen you up, because I don't want you to be tense when I tie you up and fuck you." He then pulled a small plastic bag out of his pants and walked over to the bathroom counter, turned on the lights, and started to lay out some lines of cocaine. There was no way on God's green earth that I was going to either do drugs or be in a room with this guy when he was fucked up on cocaine.

He had his back to me as he laid out the lines. I got up quickly, unlocked the door, and ran outside. I didn't care how bizarre I looked, I just wanted to get away from this guy. I ran up to the office. I was going to ask the clerk to call the police. At the moment

I entered the office, I saw the guy run bare ass out of the motel room. He saw me in the office, ducked back into the room, and then raced back out with his clothes in hand. He jumped into his car, started it up, and drove off stark naked into the night.

The clerk, a small Oriental man, leered at me.

"You one of those hos from the Queen Mary! You betta get out! I call the police now!"

I ran back into the room, grabbed my dress, wig, and purse. I raced down the alley behind the motel and hid behind a dumpster in back of a restaurant. I quickly put my dress and wig back on and started walking the few blocks back to the Queen Mary. My heart was racing. I took my heels off so I could walk faster. I then realized that I forgot my panties because my male equipment was bulging out the front of my tight dress. Fuck, I thought, I hope a cop doesn't see me. Sliding my purse over the bulge, I sped back to the parking lot. I didn't see Mr. Psycho around, so I got into my car and went home.

As soon as I walked in the door I cleaned myself up and called a locksmith to get the cuffs off of my wrist. He laughed like it was something he had seen before. After he left, I fell apart. I realized that I could've been killed in that hotel room. It was then I decided that my cross-dressing had gone far enough. I had another drink and fell asleep.

The next day I bagged up all of my women's clothes and transvestite pornography. I gave whatever was usable and decent to the Salvation Army and I ditched all of the other stuff in a big dumpster at a business park. I then drove around for hours in a haze. It was a Saturday and I didn't know what to do with myself. I went to a phone booth and made a few calls. I wound up meeting an old friend at a singles bar I used to hang out at. It felt good to have a couple of drinks and look at women.

CAN A MAN QUIT CROSS-DRESSING?

When Ed [Yvonne] threw away his feminine paraphernalia and renounced his cross-dressing, he was engaging in a ritual seen periodically within CD circles. Called *purging,* it is a radical, and often expensive, attempt to free one's self from the Black Lace Prison. But does purging work? Can a man escape from the Black Lace Prison? Can he truly quit cross-dressing?

Even if Ed were able to give up cross-dressing altogether, his other problems would not go away. If anything, his problems would be heightened to the extent that he had been using cross-dressing to mask them. One could easily argue that his drinking and sexual promiscuity pose much more serious problems than his cross-dressing.

Ed's homophobia is also bizarre. He "doesn't have anything against them," but he's not one of them—particularly since he doesn't have anal sex. Here again emerges the CD notion that one is not gay or bisexual because he dresses like a woman during sex with a man. Ed also seems to feel that limiting his activity to oral sex is further evidence of his nonhomosexuality. In addition to his other problems, Ed is simply in denial about his sexual inclinations.

It is tempting to liken the problem of maladaptive cross-dressing to alcoholism. How valid is the comparison? While it has some interesting parallels to alcoholism, I don't think it approaches the severity of chemical dependency. On the other hand, a substance abuser doesn't have to renounce sexual gratification to achieve sobriety, so cross-dressing may present an equally great obstacle in this respect.

The similarity between the two is strongest when we understand that both behaviors exhibit the classic double-bind that can turn any pleasure into a living hell: Drinking and cross-dressing are forms of pleasurable intoxication that can become self-destructive if not understood and handled responsibly. Like a Chinese finger trap, the walls of the Black Lace Prison are held together by the tension of pain and pleasure pulling against each other: The harder one tries to quit cross-dressing, the more resistance he encounters from his sexual desire.

Any pleasure can be dangerous when it is used to numb emotional or physical pain. It is important to note here the difference between escapism and numbness, because many CDs refer to cross-dressing as an escape. I define escapism as a conscious, temporal release from stress. Escapism is a mere diversion. It is the temporary enjoyment of a pleasurable activity with the full knowledge that the stresses of life will still be there after the activity is finished.

Conversely the attempt to achieve perpetual numbness is a self-destructive effort to ignore, deny, or avoid facing the stresses of life. An alcoholic is a classic example of someone trying to become perpetually, pleasurably numb. Such a person feels intense emotional or physical pain and drinks in order to gain the intoxicated numbness that he believes will insulate him from his problems.

But the drink wears off and the problems soon return. Because the alcoholic is either unable or unwilling to deal with his problems, he drinks again. The problems return, and worse, hangovers and guilt now accompany them. He drinks again and, before long, requires yet more alcohol to achieve the desired effect. Soon he is drunk or hung over all of the time, and drink has itself become his new, overwhelming problem.

Cross-dressing gives the CD emotional and sexual pleasure, and so he develops a craving to repeat the act. How the CD handles his cravings will determine whether his cross-dressing becomes a problem. If he insists that his cravings be fulfilled no matter the cost, then his cross-dressing will indeed become a problem—to himself and others. If he realizes that, as with anything else in life, there are limits and that he will need to compromise, then he will probably be able to successfully integrate cross-dressing into his life.

If a CD's cravings represent an attempt to escape stress, then his cross-dressing may take on the air of desperation seen in alcoholism. A key mistake made by such a CD is when he starts to believe that only cross-dressing is desirable and that everything else in his life is undesirable. This decision prevents him from integrating the behavior into his life. Instead, he develops a divided life in which cross-dressing is on one side and everything else is on the other. Everything and everyone that doesn't support his behavior becomes a burden or an antagonist. Yet, to the dysfunctional CD, the male self is the analogue of the drunkard's sobriety: He desperately needs it, but he is terrified to confront it.

The dysfunctional CD knows that cross-dressing is both his curse and his salvation. He believes that it is at the core of his problems, but since it gives him extreme emotional and sexual pleasure, he knows that he can't give it up. Nevertheless, he may occasionally engage in the ritual of purging. While purging has symbolic value, it has no lasting effect—the CD has not in any way confronted his problems.

I know of instances in which the wives of CDs have demanded that their husbands stop cross-dressing or face divorce. I also know of cases where a therapist has pronounced a CD sexually neurotic and warned him to quit cross-dressing if he is to get his life back together. Are such demands reasonable?

I don't think it's possible to give up cross-dressing, for the simple reason that I believe it's a part of the CD's core sexual orientation. It's not a habit like smoking, and it can be compared to drinking only in the sense that it can become a problem. I personally don't know of anyone who has ever "quit" cross-dressing permanently. But for that matter, I don't know of anyone who has ever permanently quit masturbating.

The CD trying to quit is his own worst enemy because his sexual desires and inner nature always remind him of what he wants. Just think about it: How hard would it be for you to renounce a form of sexual expression that you not only enjoyed, but was a part of your identity? How hard would it be for you to quit thinking of yourself in the way in which you've always thought about yourself?

If a heterosexual is having sexual problems, a therapist never asks him to renounce heterosexuality as part of his treatment. Instead, the therapist might suggest that he give up certain hurtful behaviors and work through the emotional problems related to those behaviors. The aim of therapy is to free a person from sexual neurosis so that he can enjoy his sexuality. The emphasis in counseling is on changing behavior rather than orientation. I think this is the superior way to consider cross-dressing within a therapeutic context.

In Ed's case, he needs professional help to untangle the web he's woven from the threads of alcoholism, self-deception, self-pity, self-indulgence, anger, poor relational skills, and dishonesty. Ed's problem isn't cross-dressing. In fact, if he were able to renounce cross-dressing, there's a good chance that he would attempt to deal with his neurotic energies through increased drinking.

Do you think that Ed would become more honest or functional in a relationship if he were indeed able to quit cross-dressing? Do you think he wouldn't commit adultery or abuse alcohol because he's not cross-dressing? Hardly. By the way, Ed's renunciation of cross-dressing lasted only three weeks. "It's in my blood," he told himself after charging $700 on his Visa to get back into the game.

LARRY'S STORY

In chapter 2 we discussed the case of Nigel, who has integrated his enjoyment of women's clothing into his life in a positive way. His wife accepts his behavior, and few obsessive tendencies surround it. He and his wife find that his fetishism occasionally enhances their sex life.

When we contrast Nigel with Larry, the young man in the following account, it becomes evident that there is more than simple fetishism at work. Larry has been cross-dressing since he was a little boy. As he tells his story, we see a young man whose lingerie fetishism reinforces his shyness, sexual inhibition, and avoidance of intimacy.

My mother's passion for clothing was probably the biggest single contributing factor to my cross-dressing. She had a fabulous wardrobe and great taste in clothes, particularly lingerie. I always wanted to be as pretty and feminine as my mother. I used to put on her perfume, silk panties, robe, high heels, and lipstick when I was alone and imagine what it would be like to be a beautiful woman.

When I was growing up, my parents owned a real estate agency and were very involved in the community. They were busy most evenings and weekends. Since they worked locally, they left me alone in the evenings. This was fine with me because it gave me plenty of time to play with my mom's clothes.

My parents were real networkers. When I was fourteen they volunteered to run the thrift shop for our church. They did this so that my dad could become an elder at our church. Once he was an elder it would help him sell even more houses; after all, who wouldn't buy a home from a church elder?

My parents thought that I could help run the thrift store to earn some pocket money and learn how a small business works. They never actually worked at the store. Instead, they did the books and paid me out of their pocket for the work I did. Ironically, my mother never once gave anything of hers to the store because, as she told my dad, "I just can't bear to part with any of my things."

(This, by the way, was the rationale that Bob used to accumulate 2,100 pairs of panties. In terms of cultural aesthetics, however, it is acceptable for men to hoard tools and sporting goods in the garage while women can hoard clothing in the closet. It seems odd when the cases are reversed, doesn't it?)

The thrift store was to give me access to a world of women's clothing for the next four years. I settled into a nice pattern during the school year. Two of the older matrons in the church would work the store while I was in school, and I would take over in the afternoons. They thought I was being a dear because I sorted and tagged most of the donated clothes—all I really wanted was first crack at the clothing in the bags.

So I didn't arouse suspicion, I had to make sure that enough clothes, shoes, and lingerie made it onto the racks. Of course, the stuff that made it onto the racks was the junk I didn't want, you know, anything in plaid, big-girl girdles, panties with droopy elastic, flannel nightgowns, industrial-strength bras, sensible shoes, and old-lady clothes that smelled like mothballs.

I started to really get into lingerie and high heels. I also began to experiment with cosmetics, and, with the help of several wigs I got from the store, I soon made a pretty good-looking girl. On Friday and Saturday nights I would tell my parents that I was going out after work to meet friends, but what I would really do was hang around in the back room and try on different outfits in front of the mirror, play with cosmetics, and masturbate. As long as I was home by eleven, I never had to worry.

Occasionally people would leave bags behind the store at night.

I found the weirdest stuff in these anonymous donations. Dirty magazines, crotchless panties, an occasional dildo, hula skirts, half-full bottles of booze, dried-out joints, real old pornography, and car parts. I once even found a stuffed owl with a Masonic emblem mounted on its breast. To save the matrons the embarrassment of unpacking an issue of *Juggs* magazine or any of the other vile cast-offs of their neighbors, I would take what I wanted and throw away the rest.

By the time I was seventeen, I had amassed an impressive collection of the best clothing, lingerie, heels, and porn. I kept my things stashed in boxes in a corner of the attic of my parent's home. The attic access was through a small door in the lower wall of a utility closet on the second floor, so the stuff I used the most I kept hidden right behind that door. I figured out a way to discreetly shim the attic door so that it couldn't be easily opened. My dad was no handyman; I never really worried about him going into the attic.

I had plenty of time alone at home to play with my things, but I always preferred playing after hours in the back room of the store because there was less chance of being caught. I never felt exactly right about what I was doing, in fact I felt guilty. I felt like I was the only person in the world who did this kind of thing. Still, when I was dressed up, being a girl felt like the best thing in the world.

Right after I graduated from high school, my parents bought a fabulous new home. It had a guest residence above the garage. My dad insisted that I take the guest residence since, as he said, "You're a young man now, and you need your privacy." This was fortunate because I was running out of places to hide things at our old house.

Unfortunately, the one and only time my mom did anything around the house was when we were moving into the new house. She decided to pack some small antiques she had in the attic of the old house. I had forgotten they were in the attic and I hadn't yet moved all of my collection.

I came home from the store and she asked me to sit down at the kitchen table. "What are all of those things doing in our attic?" she demanded.

I looked down at the floor. I couldn't think of a plausible answer.

165 • THE BLACK LACE PRISON

"Have you been stealing those things from the thrift store?" she demanded.

"I bought them," I said in utter embarrassment.

"Why, Larry?" she asked.

I confessed to her that I liked to wear women's clothing and begged her not to tell my father. My mom looked up at the ceiling for a moment.

"I've been worried that you had a thing for my clothes ever since you were a little boy. I've noticed over the years when my clothes had been moved, but I guess that I just wanted to ignore it. It was you getting into my things, wasn't it?"

I nodded.

"You know," she continued, "this need of yours to wear women's clothing is bad enough without you having to risk ruining your parents' reputation. I mean, what if you got caught? Our business would go down the drain. I want you to quit working at the store immediately."

I asked her what we should do with all the stuff in the attic.

"I'll take care of it," she replied. "I also think you should see a psychologist."

"Why?" I asked defensively.

"Because this isn't normal. Besides, I'm worried that you're a homosexual. Is that why you like to wear women's clothing?"

I insisted that it wasn't.

"Then why don't you ever date girls? Why haven't you ever dated any of my friends' daughters that I've introduced to you?"

"Because I didn't like any of them," I replied.

"You didn't like Andrea? Andrea is very cute and you know for a fact that she has a crush on you."

"I like Andrea for a friend. I just haven't met any girls that I like," I responded.

"I'm just worried that you're gay," she said, trying to hold back tears.

"Mom, if I were gay, I would hang around with Thomas Kemper and all of his friends," I said, hoping to strike a sensitive nerve. Thomas Kemper was the son of my mom's best friend.

"Thomas Kemper is not gay," she asserted.

"He is majorly gay," I insisted. "He openly let it be known that he was going to take his boyfriend Derek to the senior prom. If the headmaster hadn't pressured his parents, he would have been there with Derek."

"That's enough," she sternly intoned. "Even if you're not gay you still need to talk to someone about this need of yours; it's simply not normal for a young man to wear women's clothing. And if you give me any difficulty I will tell your father about this. Do you understand?"

I had to agree to counseling. Within three days, my vast lingerie, clothing, and magazine collection was gone. My mom had taken it all to a big Salvation Army store in a nearby town. Not surprisingly, she dumped all of it behind the store at night. It filled eight big trash bags that she had to jam into her Mercedes. She wouldn't talk to me for months afterward.

We soon moved into the new house; I started college and began therapy. I was so stressed by it all. It felt like my mother had given an entire part of my life to the Salvation Army. I thought of sneaking some of my mother's panties, but I hated her so much at that point that the thought of wearing anything of hers sickened me. Though she never talked to me directly about my cross-dressing again, my mother hovered over me to make sure I kept my appointments with the therapist. It made me so angry. The one time I missed an appointment, she withheld my allowance and took the keys to my car for a week.

The therapist was a complete space cadet. One time she had me put on nothing but a pair of panties for a session. She then brought in one of her female grad students in a bra and panties. She said that she wanted me to "experience the difference between a real woman and her underwear." When I told her that I felt humiliated by what she was doing, she said that I was finally getting in touch with the deep psychic wound to my male ego. Jesus, I thought, I just like to wear women's clothes—what's the big deal about some "deep psychic wound"?

Despite her efforts to cure me, I was desperate to rebuild my collection. I started driving to other towns to scrounge through secondhand stores. I never told my therapist about this. Instead, I told her that I had begun a relationship with a girl. I wasn't in fact in a relationship with anybody, but I figured that it might convince her that I was being sufficiently normal. I was finally able to end my sessions with her about a year later.

I lived in the guest residence at my parents' home all through college. In the four years I lived in it, my dad only came up twice. My mother avoided the place like it was roach infested. The guest house gave me the privacy to indulge my fascination with women's clothes and lingerie.

After college I took a job with a big corporation and moved to Chicago so that I could get away from my mother; she was always brooding whenever she was around me. I lived in a small apartment by myself and didn't have any friends. I would cross-dress most nights. On weekends I started to scout the area thrift stores for women's clothes.

One day I thought to myself, Why am I going into secondhand stores? I'm making pretty good money, I can afford to buy new things. What a difference the new clothes and lingerie in the big department stores made! I imagined myself as a sort of Cinderella who always wore hand-me-downs—and now I got to have the nice, new clothes and glass slippers.

I went crazy with my Visa card. I couldn't control myself; I was suddenly more obsessed than I'd ever been with women's clothing—especially lingerie. At the end of a three-month period I had purchased almost $3,500 in clothing and cosmetics. I slowed down after that, but I guess I still spend about $300 a month on women's clothing. It makes me happy to go out and buy clothes, and I can afford it—so why not?

One day after work I went to a happy hour with some of my coworkers. I met this girl, call her Greta, and we started going out. She wound up liking me much more than I liked her. We eventually had sex. It was my first time and it seemed so dreary, messy, and embarrassing. I just couldn't understand what the big deal about sex was, especially since it didn't approach the feelings I had when I dressed.

I told Greta that I was into lingerie in hopes that she would dump me. But she didn't. She said she understood. She even tried to become involved in my interest, but it always felt so intrusive. We would go out to look at lingerie at the mall and she just didn't understand. She would always ask me, "Why do you need to have so much lingerie?"

I asked her if we could both wear panties when we made love. She agreed, and I was glad because it was the only way that I could really enjoy sex. But then she got to where she didn't want to have the panties involved all of the time. I tried to oblige her, but I didn't like sex without panties. I felt so awkward about the matter that I finally stopped bringing up the topic and started to avoid the whole sex thing. Greta eventually broke up with me because she said she needed someone who loved her and not her underwear. I was so humiliated that I haven't dated since then—and that was about two years ago.

When I want sex with a woman, I've found that it's so much easier to hire a prostitute. I've met one hooker in particular, Glenda, who really knows how to give me what I want. Glenda dresses me in lingerie and tells me how cute I look. She allows me pick out the lingerie I want her to wear, and then masturbates me with a sexy pair of panties, or, if I want, we have sex while we both wear lingerie. If I ever get married, it would be to a woman like Glenda.

I'm perfectly content with my life and have started to dress up around the house when I'm not at work. I also joined a sort of lingerie-fetish club that I found out about through a computer bulletin board. We get together on line and talk about lingerie and discuss the latest pieces from our respective collections. It's such a big relief to be around people who share my interest.

Larry's behavior is quite distinct from Bob's, the man with 2,100 pairs of panties, or from Nigel's, the Australian. Both Bob and Nigel are married, have children, interact well with others, and have enjoyable sexual relations with their wives. While Bob's panty collection is psychologically interesting, it doesn't form the center of his life. Larry's life, however, revolves around women's clothing.

Larry's cross-dressing serves as a way to avoid intimacy and involvement with other people. Larry is compulsive about buying clothes and lingerie and typically spends several hours per week shopping. He has set up a spreadsheet on his PC that tells him the description, cost, date, manufacturer, and store where he has purchased every item since starting his "new" collection.

He has also re-created from memory the "old" lingerie collection that his mother confiscated and loaded that onto a spreadsheet. His goal is to try to duplicate as many items from that collection as he can. "It would be the ultimate form of revenge against my mother," he confides.

For both Ed and Larry, cross-dressing is maladaptive. Should they try to quit? No, for "trying to quit" would be as futile as the person who "tries to quit" being heterosexual after a failed marriage. It doesn't logically follow that because one fails in marriage, heterosexuality is to blame. Similarly, it doesn't follow that because one is a maladaptive CD, cross-dressing is to blame. In both cases, the issue is not about one's sexual identity. Instead, the issue is one of behavior.

Sexuality does not exist in a vacuum. The idea that cross-dressing somehow exists in a vacuum is perhaps the most common misapprehension people have about it. Wives and girlfriends sometimes assume that cross-dressing is a separate, detachable part of a man's behavior, just as many CDs assume that the behavior somehow exists independently within their psyche. But this is simply not true. Cross-dressing is part of the fabric of the CD's personality.

To successfully integrate marriage into one's life requires a tremendous amount of communication, compromise, and commitment. It should not be surprising to discover that the struggle to intelligently integrate cross-dressing into one's life requires these same qualities. And this is where many CDs make a crucial mistake, for they think cross-dressing should be all play and no work. On the contrary, it takes a hell of a lot of work to handle cross-dressing.

When a CD doesn't handle the personal and relational issues that surround his cross-dressing he loses control of both it and his life in general. This is exactly the same thing that happens when a person doesn't handle any important life issue.

The question in dysfunctional cross-dressing shouldn't be whether or not one can, or must, quit. Rather, the challenge is to transform one's relationship to cross-dressing so that it becomes an integrated aspect of one's life. To do so takes a strong desire to work through a host of seemingly unrelated problems.

Acceptance is the most powerful gesture toward transformation that the CD and those close to him, especially the woman in his life, can make. Acceptance of one's self, and acceptance of one's self by another, opens the gates of the Black Lace Prison. However, acceptance can only come with honesty, negotiation, and compromise. The CD must try to understand and accommodate the feelings and needs of those around him. Likewise, those around the CD must understand that his feelings and needs are not going to disappear or change.

Acceptance is often a matter of negotiation. In my case, my wife and I agreed that I would keep my cross-dressing away from our home and children, and that I would limit it to those occasions when I travel or go to a PPOC meeting. This means that I typically dress only two to four evenings per month.

Because my wife and I live on a budget like so many others, we agreed that we would both have an allowance each week, and that if I wanted to spend mine on women's clothing or cosmetics, she wouldn't express a negative opinion since it was my money to do with as I pleased. Is this everything I had wanted? No, for I would prefer to dress more frequently and spend more money, but it's a workable solution within my marriage.

I'm willing to accept that part of adult life is realizing that one will never have everything one wants. Yet many CDs feel that they are being woefully deprived if they cannot freely cross-dress. But it is immature to expect that just because one immensely enjoys something, others must always accommodate that enjoyment.

It just doesn't work that way. It doesn't matter if it's fishing, bowling, stamp collecting, dancing, partying, or cross-dressing. The fact is that one must accept the constraints of time, money, and the feelings of partners when they're in a relationship. And besides, there are few things more insufferable than a pouting CD, and nothing worse than an intolerant, angry spouse.

Cross-dressing can be perverse or it can be an enjoyable and integrated aspect of a man's life. Taking personal responsibility for one's life is what makes the difference. For the CD who suspects that his behavior is not entirely healthy, it is important to seek professional help. And for the CD who is honestly struggling to integrate his behavior into his everyday life, it is vital to never surrender one's dignity to the prejudices or hostilities of others. Great skill, courage, and determination are required to surmount life's obstacles and find one's true self.

8

A DAY IN THE LIFE OF THE
TRANSGENDER COMMUNITY

A s the fog lifts on a spring morning, the shimmering waters of
the blue Pacific can be seen from the hillside homes in pic-
turesque Capistrano Beach, California. Sandy Thomas, a well-
known publisher of CD fantasy literature and an archivist of CD
culture, drives to the post office to pick up the morning mail. Orders
from CDs all over the world pour in to his post office box. With over
150 titles in his catalogue, Sandy Thomas has charted the fantasy life
of the CD as has no other. In doing so he has boldly redefined what
it is to be a *sissy*.

At midafternoon in fashionable Sherman Oaks, California, John,
an independent film editor, makes his way into a very special store.
The store is Lydia's TV Fashions, a boutique that caters to CDs. Lydia's
offers wigs, breast forms, lingerie, shoes, dresses, and CD magazines
to both their retail and mail-order customers. The store has been
providing these valuable supplies to the CD community in confidence for almost twenty years.

John is looking for a pair of ankle-strap heels to go with a new dress
he just bought at a department store. "I don't mind buying most of
my female clothing in department stores," he remarks, "but when it
comes to lingerie and shoes, I just can't do it. I feel like everyone in

the store is staring at me. So I go to Lydia's to shop for those things. I can also come here when I'm dressed up, and I like the fact that I can try on a dress or a pair of shoes before I buy them. You can't do that in a department store!"

No you can't, John, and that's why the retailers throughout the United States and Europe who cater to the CD have been able to earn a decent living. There are also a host of regular retailers who have become wise to the fact that CDs will bring in many extra dollars to their establishments if they're made welcome. What normally happens is that a CD will start to shop regularly at a friendly store—usually a small boutique—and will eventually tell the owner, usually a woman, about his interest. She assures him that he is welcome and his business is appreciated.

After a while the CD will ask if his friends can shop at the store. The owner normally agrees on the condition that they do not shop while dressed as women. This is appropriate so that the regular clientele is not disturbed. Another solution innovative retailers have offered is to have a special after-hours sale for CDs. At these events CDs can come dressed and try on clothes to their heart's content. Many of these shopping events have become affairs offering hors d'oeuvres, drinks, and a fashion show featuring the retailer's selection.

At the same time that John is visiting Lydia's, another CD, this one a salesman in the electronics industry, is visiting a bookstore a scant three miles away in neighboring Van Nuys. The bookstore, Mags Inc., is a retailer and mail-order house that sells CD fantasy literature. Mags Inc. is in a small commercial building next to a travel agency on Van Nuys Boulevard.

Mags Inc. boasts the most complete selection of CD literature in the country, including many European titles that are almost impossible to find in the United States. Mags Inc.'s mail-order business is formidable. Its highly confidential mailing list is rumored to consist of over five thousand names.

In Provincetown, Massachusetts, Fantasia Fair, the oldest annual CD convention in the nation, is in the third day of its thirtieth annual meeting. Fantasia Fair lasts four days and features prominent speakers in the field of gender research and education; workshops on the medical aspects of taking female hormones for preoperative trans-sexuals; classes on feminine deportment and grooming; and an awards ceremony Saturday night to honor those who have labored on behalf of the transgendered community. About two hundred CDs, most of them from the East Coast, attend, and many bring their wives.

In Houston, Phyllis Randolph Frye and others are presenting the International Conference on Transgender Law and Employment Policy, an annual symposium on the law as it relates to cross-dressers, transgenderists, and transsexuals. The purpose of this unique event is to discuss the state of current laws as they relate to the transgendered and to help to formulate more enlightened laws that affirm the rights of such people.

That evening in San Francisco, a stockbroker attends a meeting of Educational TV Channel. ETVC is a CD support group with over six hundred members in the Bay Area. This meeting marks the first time that the stockbroker has ventured out in public dressed as a woman. Also in attendance at this meeting is "Joan," a member of the PPOC board of directors.

Joan, a Vietnam veteran with twenty-five missions as a crewman aboard a B-52 under his belt, is visiting San Francisco to finalize details for a joint PPOC/ECTV meeting here next year. Joan's wife, Barbara, a stunning femme fatale, accompanies him to the ETVC meeting.

Barbara, sensing the stockbroker's nervousness, strikes up a conversation with him. Grateful to be able to talk to a real woman about his cross-dressing, the stockbroker is soon pouring out his heart to Barbara. It is a story that she has heard often from CDs. He wonders whether he'll ever find a woman who will love him. Barbara listens patiently and reassures him that there is a woman out there who will accept and love him as he is.

Later that night, an off-duty air traffic controller is parked in front of his home computer in a quiet suburb of Chicago. After making sure that his wife and children are sleeping soundly, the man furtively logs on to Cross-Connection, a Los Angeles–based bulletin board that has become a leading resource for the nation's transgendered community. In addition to being a TG bulletin board, Cross-Connection is also an Internet server for those wishing to cruise the transgendered boards worldwide. There, the cruiser can gain a confidential introduction to the fascinating and mysterious world of men who, like himself, enjoy dressing as women.

The man is a closet CD who is thinking of joining a Chicago area CD club. He read about Cross-Connection in *Cross-Talk*, a magazine devoted to current affairs within the CD community. In the pages of *Cross-Talk* this man discovered that he was not alone, that many thoughtful and intelligent men cross-dress, and that many activities are available to the contemporary CD.

The modern world of cross-dressing has become organized, articulate, and adventuresome. Seemingly every day we see one of its members on a talk show. That the general interest in the topic has expanded is evidenced by the proliferation of movies and television shows that feature CDs, and magazine articles, books, and research papers on the subject. How did all of this get started?

VIRGINIA PRINCE: THE FOUNDER OF THE MODERN CROSS-DRESSING MOVEMENT

What is not widely known—even in CD circles—is that the modern CD movement began in 1929 aboard an ocean liner in the North Atlantic. The vessel was the Cunard steamship *Transylvania*. There sixteen-year-old Charles Prince, who was traveling with his parents to Europe where his physician father was to attend a medical conference, first realized how much he wanted to dress as a woman.

The occasion was a ball on the final night of the crossing. The wife of one of the other doctors aboard tried to coax young Charles to attend the ball dressed as a girl. Charles refused out of a sense of propriety, but the experience triggered an avalanche of feeling within the young man that was to later form the basis of the modern CD movement.

Young Charles Prince would be haunted by that moment aboard the *Transylvania* for years to come. He continually found himself returning to that moment and wishing that he had dressed as a girl that night. His longing drove him to collect a private, hidden wardrobe of women's clothing. Soon Charles grew tired of his closet and began venturing out onto the streets of his native Los Angeles dressed as a young woman.

Prince's college years were filled with the hard work that culminated in a Ph.D. in biochemistry. But even his scholarly labors could not deter him from his love of things feminine. He continued his forays out into public and, when the opportunity presented itself, attended costume parties dressed as a woman.

When Prince married, he renounced cross-dressing. His wife knew nothing of his interests, and he vowed to abstain for the sake of his marriage. But his effort was futile, for he soon found himself back-sliding into the pleasures of feminine finery. He kept this secret from his wife for several years.

After his university work, Prince accepted a staff position with the University of California at San Francisco's medical school. There he had the occasion to see a CD who had been presented at grand rounds. When the presenting psychiatrist was giving the psychometrics of the patient, Prince was astonished. He literally thought for a moment that the psychiatrist was describing him because, ironically, the patient was of the same age and attended the same junior college as had Prince.

In the following weeks another CD was presented. Prince tarried after the presentation to speak with the CD. The two wound up having a lengthy discussion in the parking lot of the university. While looking through a photo album that the CD had in the car, Prince spied the name and phone number of a Berkeley area CD, one "Louise Lawrence," on one of the photos. Desperate to meet another CD, Prince called Louise Lawrence and arranged a meeting at her house. Prince confessed his desires to her and had soon made a friend. His contact with Louise enabled him to meet other CDs, and for the first time in his life Prince realized that others shared that same longing for the feminine that he had experience that night on the *Transylvania*.

In the early 1940s Charles and his wife moved back to Los Angeles, where he took a position with a pharmaceutical manufacturing firm. It was during this time that he finally told his wife that he was a cross-dresser. She did not take the news well. Nevertheless, they worked out an arrangement whereby Charles would occasionally dress while his wife removed herself to the back of their home.

In a remarkable display of disclosure for the late 1940s, Prince also told both his father and a male colleague about his cross-dressing. His physician father suggested that Charles obtain a medical evaluation to determine if he was lacking in male hormones. Charles's revelation to his father strained their relationship, though the two remained on reasonably good terms.

In 1948 Prince left the pharmaceutical firm and with a partner started a chemical manufacturing firm in Westwood, California. The business allowed Prince to freely pursue his cross-dressing interests without fear of incurring an employer's displeasure; it also provided him with an upper-middle-income lifestyle.

Charles Prince's wife grew increasingly distraught with her husband's behavior. Convinced that he was a homosexual, she filed for divorce in 1950. The divorce attracted the attention of the local press and became something of a cause célèbre in area newspapers. The story was picked up by the Associated Press and broadcast nationally. Prince endured the humiliating exposure and publicity concerning his personal life and stoically carried on with his affairs.

All the while, Prince had been building a network of CD friends. Using the name "Muriel," Prince got an apartment following his divorce and began circulating in the CD underground in Los Angeles. In the early fifties, Muriel and her CD friends met at "Johnny's Place," which was the Long Beach apartment of a fellow CD. The idea of producing a publication devoted to cross-dressing often came up in conversation there. Prince decided to pursue this project, and *Transvestia* was born. In its first incarnation, *Transvestia* was simply a mimeographed newsletter that soon flopped.

One evening while at his parents' home for supper, Prince met their new housekeeper, an Englishwoman whom he will only refer to as "D." He soon struck up a platonic relationship with "D" and told her of his interest in cross-dressing. She was receptive and showed a great deal of interest; the two eventually married.

Comfortable in a supportive relationship, Prince turned his attentions back to the world of publishing. Reviving his earlier, failed idea for a CD publication, a more professional version of *Transvestia* appeared in January 1960 as a small offset magazine. *Transvestia* featured reader-written stories, fictional stories, cartoons, photographs, poetry, ads seeking pen pals, editorials, and analysis related to transvestism. One hundred issues were published before the publication ceased. Reprints of some of the old issues are still available through Sandy Thomas Publications. These vintage issues provide a quaint view into an earlier period of cross-dressing. *Transvestia* was devoted to a lofty purpose. As Prince stated in 1963:

> *Transvestia* is published by, for, and about Transvestites for the purpose of providing a center about which people in the field may gather. Its pages will provide Entertainment for the initiated; Education for those who see evil where none exists; and Expression of opinion both lay and professional. Discussion, sharing ideas and experiences all lead to greater understanding of any facet of human behavior.
>
> *Transvestia* seeks to provide information both to and about Transvestites and Transvestism in order to broaden the understanding of this form of personality expression, not only among those interested in it, but by friends and relatives who may find themselves indirectly involved.
>
> *Transvestia* also serves as a means of gathering information as well as disseminating it. Medical science has no adequate means of contacting and interviewing enough Transvestites who are reasonably well adjusted to their problem and not complicated by other psychosocial behavior patterns to form any well considered opinions about the subject. This magazine has and will continue to provide research material to further the understanding of Transvestism by psychiatrists, psychologists, sociologists, lawyers, jurists, and police officials.

The success of *Transvestia* led Prince to start two other publications, the *FemmeMirror* and *Clipsheet*. The *FemmeMirror* was a smaller publication printed in alternate months. Its run initially lasted for forty-four issues. It appeared erratically for several years, but now it is published monthly as the official membership magazine of *Tri-Ess*. *Clipsheet* grew out of Prince's longtime habit of keeping a scrapbook of CD-related articles she found in newspapers and magazines. *Clip-

sheet was just that—a bimonthly collection of news clippings that had been sent in by alert CD readers from all over the world. It was published until 1972. *Transvestia* remained in publication until September 1977, when the last official issue—a short autobiography by Virginia Prince—rolled off the press.

In the late 1950s Muriel Prince changed her name. Tired of being likened to the cigar, the CD formerly known as Muriel Prince became not an undecipherable symbol but rather the more prosaic Virginia Prince—the name under which she would become a legend.

In 1961 Virginia Prince began the world's first known CD support group. Hose and Heels met in a small church building in the vicinity of Sunset and Bronson in Hollywood. With the success of the club came the desire to expand the club concept into other cities. A national organization was launched in 1962 by Prince and other CDs. Called Phi Pi Epsilon, which stood for Full Personality Expression (FPE), this CD organization would found chapters in many cities throughout the world. Hose and Heels was accordingly renamed the Alpha Chapter of FPE.

Prince is often asked about the origins of the name of her first CD club, Hose and Heels. As she explained it to me, the name stemmed from the fact that CDs in that day and age faced the very real prospect of arrest if the police caught them cross-dressed. Prince also had a significant fear that an undercover vice officer would attempt to infiltrate her gathering of CDs. Hence, she asked each member to come to the meeting with two bags. In the first bag was to be a snack for the group. In the second bag was to be a pair of women's hose and heels.

A meeting would begin with a discussion followed by snacks. Afterward, Prince would ask everyone to take off their male shoes and slip into their hose and heels. The moment of truth came, according to Prince, when each man slipped on his heels, for she reasoned that a true CD would have heels that fit properly whereas a vice officer might well overlook this important detail. Also, the act of putting on hose and heels was a form of initiation and bonding, for it was an admission of one's true desires to other CDs.

Prince's paranoia was well founded. Well into the early 1970s, the Los Angeles Police Department, and other police agencies throughout the United States, enforced the statutes against men who cross-dressed. Female impersonators who performed onstage were required to comply with these laws by doing such things as wearing signs or buttons that read I'M A BOY, or wearing their male clothing under their female costume.

The legal oppression of the CD was carried out not by the jack-booted government thugs of NRA infamy, but rather by the dour, antisexual, crewcutted Joe Fridays of *Dragnet.* The mores of the period were staunchly against any manifestation of homosexuality or sexual aberration in general. It is well established that police agencies routinely harassed gay men and CDs well into the 1970s.

Despite what may have happened in the past, it is almost unheard of these days for a CD to be harassed by the police. In fact, in those cases where a CD is arrested he usually has it coming to him. The occasional CD will delude himself into thinking that he is passable enough to try on bras in the dressing room of a department store. This usually results in an arrest for disguising oneself for an illegal purpose, namely voyeurism. Even if the CD protests that he is completely innocent, the fact is that women are justified in thinking that a CD is nothing but a voyeur when he trespasses into locations where they are likely to be unclothed.

Every so often a CD will be nabbed for shoplifting, soliciting prostitution, or driving under the influence and will have to spend a night in jail enduring the insults and/or advances of his fellow inmates. Being arrested while dressed as a woman can be a horrible experience, yet avoidable if a CD carefully considers his actions and the risks they might pose.

Prince himself attracted the attention of the postal authorities in the early 1960s for his publishing activities. The authorities were not pleased that *Transvestia* was being sent through the mails, thinking that it bordered on pornography. They kept an eye on Prince and his operation. Finally, in 1964, Prince was arrested on federal charges of sending sexually explicit letters through the United States mail.

The charges were unrelated to *Transvestia.* It seems that Prince had been sending private correspondence of an erotic nature to a person whom he believed to be a woman. The "woman" was in fact a man who was already under investigation by the postal authorities. Prince thus became the unwitting victim of a perverted man who used a false pretense to entice other men to send him lurid love letters. The postal inspector didn't see it this way and pressed charges. Prince agreed to plead guilty to the federal charges and received a suspended five-year prison sentence. This episode was to be a defining event in her life.

Prince, who had freely cross-dressed in public up until this time, now faced the possibility of prison time if arrested for any crime, including the crime of cross-dressing. Her dilemma thus became one of finding a legal way to cross-dress. A request from her attorney offered the perfect solution. He asked if she would come and lecture at his Kiwanis Club. She agreed and gained a pretext to legally appear in public dressed as a woman. One invitation led to another, and soon Prince was in wide demand to speak on the subject of cross-dressing.

Due to the flimsiness of the original charges, the court released Prince from probation within five months. But by this time the die was cast; Virginia was beginning to add radio and television appearances to her already busy speaking schedule. In 1965 she became the first CD ever to appear on television.

For fifty-five-year-old Prince 1968 was a pivotal year. He sold his half of the business to his partner and was able to retire with a decent income. He attended a nude encounter group in which the other attendees were able to accept him as a woman despite his anatomy. Their acceptance profoundly affected him. As he said of the experience in his autobiography:

> If others could accept my womanhood, when they could also see my maleness, why should I have any difficulty accepting it myself? And if I could, why should I feel guilty about it? So the experience had finally put an end to the long years of guilt that we all [referring to CDs] have experienced. From that day on, my self-identity was between my ears, not between my legs, where, unfortunately, it remains for most people, including TVs.

What emerged from this experience was Prince's unshakable conviction that gender, or masculinity and femininity, are not dependent upon one's born sex. From 1968 on, Prince determined that he would live full time as a woman. And what use was there for *Charles* Prince anyway? For by 1968 *Virginia* Prince had become the international lecturer and a widely recognized authority on cross-dressing. The organization she had helped found, FPE—which would later become Tri-Ess—had also grown tremendously by adding chapters throughout the United States and Europe.

Having achieved full self-acceptance, that most valuable aspect of human maturity, she became free to devote her energies without the enervating effects of guilt. It is interesting to note that Prince's autobiography before 1968 recounts a life of struggle; after 1968 it becomes a travelogue that spans the continents in the service of the CD. Prince has since continued to work tirelessly for the cause of cross-dressing. Lecturing, speaking, traveling, and writing, Prince at age eighty-two would exhaust many a younger CD.

CRACKS IN THE DAM

For all his success, Prince was not without his troubles. In the 1950s his first wife contested his visiting rights with his son in a messy court battle, accusing him publicly of being an unfit parent, a cross-dresser, and a masturbator. His wife's Southern Baptist attorney, when challenged by Prince in open court to admit whether he had ever masturbated, remarked that he may have done so as a teenager and backed down from this line of questioning. Prince was able to retain his visiting rights.

An employee of Chevalier Publications, Prince's company that published *Transvestia,* claimed in a divorce action that Prince had conspired with the man's wife to deny him partial ownership of the company. The case was later dismissed, but only after much travail and expense.

Prince's second wife filed a divorce action in 1964 in which she alleged that Prince concealed and squandered marital assets. An extensive accounting of his personal and business finances was undertaken. It revealed no improprieties.

In 1974 Prince resigned from the Alpha Chapter of FPE after she came under heavy criticism for using the organization's mailing list in a manner that many members felt violated their privacy. She denied having violated any confidences, but the group was convinced otherwise. She received a de facto vote of no confidence when not a single person rose to her defense at a meeting in which the matter was debated. Though she tendered her resignation on the spot from the club she had founded fifteen years earlier, she retained her role as a member of the board of FPE.

Perhaps the most scathing criticism of Prince centers around Tri-Ess's decision to exclude bisexual and homosexual CDs from membership. While this decision was not made solely by Prince, some in the CD community think that it nevertheless reflects her alleged homophobia. Others think that it is hypocritical for heterosexual CDs to discriminate against bisexual or gay CDs.

Prince defends the decision to limit the scope of the club to the heterosexual CD on the basis that a club cannot be everything to everybody. Moreover, Prince feels that the wives of CDs might misconstrue what their husbands really wanted if there were gay drag queens and bisexual CDs soliciting other men at the meetings. Despite this rationale, the perception of both Prince and Tri-Ess as homophobic and parochial has been a public relations problem.

Prince has also been criticized within the CD community for being dictatorial, arrogant, and dogmatic. At her worst, she is all of these things. But at her best, she is an intelligent, fearless force for good in the CD community. Prince has been a most unusual pioneer in a realm of the human psyche that few have ever explored. Her contributions to the world of male cross-dressing are unquestionable, and despite her flaws, she remains the acknowledged founder of the modern CD movement. In her twilight years she remains as strong, clear minded, and devoted as ever to helping the CD establish his place in the world.

OTHER MAJOR GROUPS IN THE TG COMMUNITY

There are three other major organizations in the U.S. TG community that are important to note. In 1976 FPE and Mamselle, a competing organization under the direction of a CD named Carol Beecroft, merged. The new organization was called the Society for the Second Self, or Tri-Ess for short. Chapters retained their FPE Greek designations. Tri-Ess is a dominant force within the CD world to this day, and Virginia Prince is still on its board. Tri-Ess currently has twenty-six chapters throughout the United States. The original chapter, Alpha, was started by Virginia in 1976 in Los Angeles and is active today.

It became clear to many in the late 1970s that while Tri-Ess was good for opening and maintaining CD clubs at the local level, its declared intention of serving only the heterosexual CD prevented it from meeting the needs of others in the transgender community. In 1978, Merrisa Sherrill Lynn, a CD, student of philosophy, and former ski instructor, founded the International Federation of Gender Education (IFGE). Lynn later explained the purpose of IFGE this way:

> The cross-dressing and transsexual phenomena have been an integral part of the human experience as long as there has been a human experience. These phenomena have manifested themselves in every society and in every walk of life throughout history, and continue to affect the lives of vast numbers of people. Yet, as common as they are, ignorance of them, and the resulting intolerance and fear, continues to cost good people their happiness, their jobs, their families, and their lives. It costs society its neighbors, its friends, and its productive citizens. The International Federation for Gender Education is dedicated to overcoming this devastating ignorance.

Accordingly, IFGE has declared its mission to become the "leading advocate and educational organization for promoting self-definition and free expression of gender identity; changing the paradigm of gender identity by recognizing the distinction between sexual orientation and gender."

IFGE is different from Tri-Ess in that it claims to represent the whole of the TG community rather than just the CD community. IFGE boasts a full-time staff who, among other things, monitor developments in medicine, psychology, and law that relate to the transgendered. It also maintains a speakers bureau to help educate the public about transgenderism; offers legal referrals to the victims of gender discrimination; and is involved in legislative issues that affect the transgendered, such as whether insurance companies or the government should pay for sexual reassignment surgery.

IFGE's most visible contribution to the TG community is *Transgender* magazine. This magazine is clearly the highest quality publication produced within the TG community in terms of depth, writing, and production values. It features articles by health care and mental health professionals, biographical pieces and interviews with various people within the community it serves, personal ads, opinions, and poetry.

Renaissance is an organization devoted to CDs. It differs from Tri-Ess in that it is an "open" group. This means that there is no membership screening or requirement that a prospective member be heterosexual. Founded in 1987 by Jo Ann Roberts, a Pennsylvania-based CD, the Renaissance organization includes four chapters and twelve affiliates.

While Renaissance is much smaller than Tri-Ess, its influence in the CD community is significant. This is largely due to the savvy of Roberts. A former aerospace industry scientist with a Ph.D. in chemical engineering, Roberts has self-published ten books and ten instructional videos on the subject of cross-dressing in the past eight years. In addition, she publishes two periodicals on the topic and sits on the national boards of AEGIS and Renaissance. Roberts is widely considered to be a voice of reason in the American TG community.

Dallas Denny, who was introduced in chapter 4, anchors the transsexual wing of the TG community through AEGIS (American Educational Gender Information Service), the organization she began in 1990. Denny, a formally trained social scientist and a post-op TS, began AEGIS after she discovered that there was no single source of reliable medical and psychological information available to the transgendered.

Working systematically to amass such a database, Denny gained renown for compiling *the* bibliography for the TG community. Containing over five thousand entries on gender-related issues, Denny's bibliography was published by Gerald, a scientific publishing house, and has made its way into universities and research centers worldwide. Denny also began the National Trans-Gender Library and Archive as a service of AEGIS. While AEGIS is keyed to helping the transsexual, its information service has become an invaluable asset to the entire TG community.

Support groups, annual conventions, and the CD nightlife have become an important part of the transgender community. Jo Anne Roberts publishes her annual *Who's Who and Resource Guide to the Transgender Community* to keep up with the movers, shakers, and vendors in this world.

This highly useful compendium informs us that within the worldwide TG community there are currently 140 clubs and organizations, 24 annual conventions, 76 newsletters and publications, 112 medical and psychological service providers specializing in transgenderism, and 200 retail and/or mail-order businesses that cater to the transgenderist. Add to this the unknown number of nightclubs and private parties that TGs frequent and you get an idea of the activities and support available to this community.

What distinguishes these many clubs and publications from each other is their particular emphasis, for they span the range from the pornographic to the religious. This diversity is often a source of contention in the TG community, yet it demonstrates the vast psychosexual dimensions of cross-dressing. If the TG community has a critical internal challenge, it is to reconcile itself to its own diversity without resorting to the self-destructive behavior in which it periodically engages.

GENDER HALLUCINATIONS

All of this talk of gender can make the transgender community a boring and contentious place. At its best, IFGE is a peerless organization that has helped to expand and improve society's consciousness about transgenderism. Like any activist organization, however, IFGE has a preachy side in which it acts as if it alone has the wisdom to superintend the gender community. This can become tiresome, especially when it begins to take the fun out of what otherwise can be a perfectly entertaining obsession. Nineteen ninety-three was a particularly bad year for IFGE when it found itself enmeshed in controversy both inside and outside the organization.

In response to the controversy, IFGE christened its yearly convention "Coming Together, Working Together" to signal to the gender
community that it was willing to listen to its critics. Some of us felt
that this was a pretense, given IFGE's overall behavior. I decided to
parody the nice brochure they had mailed out, and the following appeared in the September 1993 edition of the redoubtable "TV Social
Register." If I were going to hold a gender convention, this is how I
would do it. I'll probably go ahead and do something like this in the
future just for the pure fun of it:

THE INTERNATIONAL FOUNDATION FOR GENDER HALLUCINATIONS
Proudly Presents Its 33rd Annual
"CONFUSED TOGETHER, IGNORING EACH OTHER"
CONVENTION
Lake Piru, California, October 3–29, 1993

Sponsor: The International Federation for Gender Hallucinations
Hosts: Sahnjay Intimate Foundations
          Mothers Against Men Fondling Themselves in Pantyhose
          The Southern California Lewdness and Lipstick Alliance

SO MUCH FUN, SO LITTLE TIME
Do you have gender hallucinations? Do you imagine yourself with
the genitals of other persons? How about breasts? Do you now, or have
you ever, had breasts? Do you dream that people are trying to break
into your house and dress you in big red lace underwear? Do you
worry that your nightly enema is slowly turning you into an hermaphrodite? Do you suspect that others are secretly watching you urinate in order to determine your true sex? Have you ever awakened to
find yourself in a strange hotel room while dressed in a velour goat costume? Was a man named Juan sleeping next to you at the time? If so,
please have him call me!

BEING IGNORED IS BLISS

You should come to our convention if you have big, scary gender hallucinations. Here you will be ignored by others too preoccupied to care. Go ahead, dress any way you like: golf pants and high heels; a raincoat and bra; pantaloons and a toupee. It really doesn't matter, because at our convention we're all too self-obsessed to be concerned with you. And that's the beauty of being ignored, isn't it? No one cares, so do whatever you want!

YOU CAN DRESS LIKE JUDY GARLAND

And you thought your mother was being cruel when she ignored you—when actually she was giving you a tremendous opportunity to do whatever you wanted. So come and celebrate apathy, indifference, and your particular gender hallucinations with us at Lake Piru.

NEWCOMERS

Novices will be feted at our wonderful "Gala of Maximum Embarrassment." Here you will pay dearly to become one of us. The featured event of the evening will be stripping you naked, shaving your head and painting it blue, tattooing a propeller on each of your butt cheeks, and then sending you screaming into the Fillmore bowling alley so we can watch the hostile reactions of the Saturday night "Bowlers for Christ" league.

LEADERSHIP

Forget it. You'll never be invited to this workshop. You're not good enough, and you'll probably never be! Sound familiar? "Leadership Through Abuse" will be the featured topic.

EDUCATIONAL PROGRAMS

What exactly are marital aids? And do they work if you're not married? See Damp Products, Inc., demonstrate its new 5hp pull-start "PleasureMate Bedroom and Lawn Tool." A nifty device with a series of removable attachments, the PleasureMate can trim bushes, set poles, blow, and clean crevices.

THE VIRGIN PRINCESS AWARD

The "VP" Lifetime Hallucination Award is given to the person who best epitomizes gender hallucinations as evidenced by his or her bizarre behavior before, during, and after institutionalization. The VP award is a beautiful stainless steel pick perfect for both performing lobotomies and chipping ice. This award makes a welcome addition to any trophy cabinet or surgical kit. It is widely coveted by health professionals and lunatics alike.

THE TRI-UNITY AWARD

A surreal statuette featuring a three-headed dragon drinking from an inverted pyramid, the Tri-Unity award is given to the individual who has perfected the three aspects of gender hallucination: Delusion, Denial, and Delirium. Could this be you?

SPIRITUAL PROGRAMS

Sister Rosie of Saint Onan's by the Sea will be our special guest speaker. Speaking on the subject "Religious Images to Meditate Upon When Alone in the Bathroom With Others," the always inspirational Sister Rosie is sure to get a big hand from our audience.

9

SOLVING THE RIDDLE OF THIS GREAT PASSION

I was alone watching television when it happened: Earthly representatives from the Kingdom of God came knocking upon my door that day in 1987. There were two of them and they were carrying small booklets. They had to be Jehovah's Witnesses. They were, and they had a big question to ask: *Did I know what truth is?*

Responding from my transvestic state of mind, I admitted that I wasn't even sure what masculinity and femininity were, let alone truth. My admission was so out of the context of their question that it confused them. They weren't sure how to respond. I think the older lady felt sorry for me, while the younger lady seemed threatened.

The older lady gave me a booklet and assured me that the Bible had the answers to all of my problems. She also offered to have some men from the local Kingdom Hall come to my home. I politely declined, not wanting to be visited by the grim males of the Watchtower Bible and Tract Society. She then thanked me for my time and, before leaving my doorstep, cleverly reminded me that Jesus was a man and that I could use him as a male role model.

Jesus? A role model for the masculinely challenged? The merits of this suggestion aside, what this woman's recommendation illustrated was the common desire to find the one answer that will explain everything. Unfortunately, such one-answer formulas are usually dogmatic and condemn everyone who doesn't agree with them.

I think I've amply demonstrated that no one answer is adequate to explain cross-dressing. However, I would like to advance two arguments in this summary chapter that, while perhaps not universal, nevertheless offer perspectives that are useful in broadening and enriching the understanding of cross-dressing. The topic sorely needs such enhancement so that it can be elevated from tragicomedy and assume its rightful place within the realm of acceptable human behavior.

The first argument proposes that an archetypal quest drives male sexuality, but that this quest takes a unique turn in the case of the CD. My purpose in presenting this first argument is to expand the definitional window of cross-dressing beyond the borders of the femme self and into the realm of the archetypal.

The second argument requires that we revisit fetishism in order to clarify the true nature of gender. My purpose in clarifying gender is to provide a preface that will allow me to place cross-dressing in the larger and more pervasive movement for cultural change.

THE ELEMENTAL ASPECT OF CROSS-DRESSING

Michael A. Lombardi-Nash, Ph.D., has given the English-speaking world a translation of the magnificent work by the German sexologist Magnus Hirschfeld, *Die Transvestiten: Eine Untersuchung über den erotishen Verkleidungsteib*, which is translated as *Transvestites: The Erotic Drive to Cross-Dress*. Published in 1910 in Berlin, Hirschfeld's book was the groundbreaking text for modern research into cross-dressing.

Flipping through the translation, I became quite aware of the special bond I have with all CDs, for we share a unique experience. Although the CDs who populate Hirschfeld's work are long dead, they could as easily have been those I have introduced you to in this book. Indeed, I was amazed at how the following quote from a turn-of-the-century CD resonated with the exact feelings I have often experienced:

I am firmly convinced that the passion for women's clothing, or rather for the absolute expression of the woman, is nothing but the desire of my feminine side to penetrate into its original reality and form. There are times when I have a direct aversion to men's clothing, when everything masculine causes in me a thorough loathing . . . when I discard from me everything about the man and put on the feminine externals, I can almost physically perceive how the false, the violence escapes out of me and disperses like a veil. Then, when, before the mirror, I see so much feminine in me, I become completely calm. I can perceive the calm quite clearly; the whole organism functions more uniformly; it is like resting after great fatigue, like the feeling of being at home in the total individuality in the role of the woman.

Even in its formal, dated language, this passage comes alive for the CD. This man's intense yearning to throw off the bonds of maleness and flow into the liberating waters of femininity where he may at last find his "original reality and form" is a desire universally felt by CDs.

Hirschfeld's work vividly shows that the experience of cross-dressing is timeless, for men have been dressing like women throughout history. The Book of Deuteronomy, written about 1450 B.C.E., is infamous within CD circles for its dread injunction:

> The woman shall not wear that which pertaineth unto a man, neither shall a man put on a woman's garment; for all that do so are an abomination unto the Lord thy God (Deut. 22:5, KJV).

In their book *Cross-Dressing, Sex, and Gender,* Doctor Vern Bullough and Dr. Bonnie Bullough discuss the historical and sociological aspects of cross-dressing, from the ancient Greek, Roman, and Jewish traditions on through to the present time. They report a fascinating account of male cross-dressing that occurred in 5 B.C.E. The subject of the account was an Assyrian king named Sardanapalus whose subjects used his cross-dressing as a pretext to launch a successful revolt against him.

As the Bulloughs and other researchers have documented, cross-dressing is not unique to our time or culture. That cross-dressing has been present throughout human history and across various cultures indicates that there is something elemental to this great passion. What is that elemental aspect?

Freud theorized that boys universally desired to possess their mothers. He further stated that this desire caused a struggle between father and son to possess the mother. Freud called this struggle the *oedipal conflict*. Oedipal theory states that in order to possess his mother, the boy must somehow conquer his father.

But what happens when the boy feels inadequate as a male? If there is no possibility of winning a contest with his father, a unique way to possess the mother would be to become her. In terms of Freud, I think that a case could be made that cross-dressing is an *esoteric* resolution of the oedipal conflict.

Essentially my theory is that a boy might cross-dress in an attempt to re-create, through the medium of his body and psyche, the image of the mother he cannot possess. To the boy, the mother represents feminine beauty, love and comfort, safety from the threatening masculinity of the father, the eroticism of a woman's body—in short, everything a weak boy wants and often cannot have.

However, Freudian theorists have typically speculated that cross-dressing is a reaction to castration anxiety, the logic being that the CD becomes a phallic woman in order to assure himself that he will not lose his penis. In my view, this supposition is weak because it does not resonate with the actual experience of CDs.

I contend that, at least from a Freudian perspective, it is the desire to possess the mother, rather than the flight from castration, that motivates the CD. Castration anxiety, as classically proposed, has never proven successful as a diagnosis for cross-dressing. Indeed, that transsexuals willingly submit to castration suggests that the desire to fully identify with the mother is stronger than the need to preserve the male identity.

The femme self of the adult CD can arguably be seen as the transvestic analogue of an adult relationship with a woman—the logic being that just as the juvenile CD became his mother, the adult CD posits a feminine self to whom he can relate emotionally and sexually. Again, this would be an arcane resolution of the adult phase of the oedipal conflict.

Still, the notion of the oedipal conflict leaves me somewhat unconvinced, as does most of Freudian psychoanalysis. I prefer to approach the issue of male sexuality by saying that all men are engaged in the search for the perfect woman—and that the perfect woman is not the mother per se.

Who, then, is she?

THE ARCHETYPE OF THE EROTIC MOTHER

I believe that the perfect woman is an archetype that I call the *Erotic Mother*, and that the search for her is a force that motivates much of men's relationships with women. The Erotic Mother is the woman whose love is both maternal and sexual. She understands a man's every need perfectly, and indulges his every sexual fantasy. The Erotic Mother is nurturing, accepting, and offers the potential for love and lust to be integrated.

Because she's archetypal, she doesn't exist in one place or as one person. Instead, elements of the Erotic Mother exist within all women. Most men search for her among her daughters, but some search for her within themselves. To the extent that a man does not comprehend the archetypal nature of his search, however, he will understand it in other terms.

Absent such an archetypal referent, CDs have typically understood their psychosexual behavior in terms of a need to express the femme self. In the world of cross-dressing, men have typically limited their self-understanding to the belief that the femme self is the best way to explain their behavior. I don't think it is, but by accepting this concept at face value, sympathetic researchers and psychologists have reinforced and legitimatized it.

While there is some merit to the notion of the femme self, I believe that the archetype of the Erotic Mother offers a much sturdier framework in which to consider cross-dressing. Yet CDs have not allowed themselves the intellectual or emotional freedom to explore cross-dressing in heroic or mythic terms. I suspect that this inability parallels the general trend in society to demythologize love and sexuality.

The demythologization of love and sexuality is a shared tragedy of twentieth-century humanity. Both love and sexuality have lost their epic potential, for by turns they have been ravaged by promiscuity, pornography, feminism, psychoanalysis, and the specter of disease. Just as the romantic yearning for the beloved has so often been reduced to a pathology, cross-dressing, stripped of an archetypal referent, has been variously reduced to a paraphilia, a sexual perversion, or a cultural aberration existing on the fringes of gender.

It seems, by default, that the only viable avenue of interpretation left to the CD is that of the feminine self. My intention in introducing the Erotic Mother into cross-dressing, then, is to expand the window of interpretation beyond the shallow perimeter of the femme self and into the domain of the archetypal—where I think much of cross-dressing belongs.

Alchemy is an attempt to transform an ordinary substance into a valuable, desirable one. In transvestic terms, the search for the Erotic Mother takes the form of alchemy, for when he cross-dresses, the CD is unconsciously attempting to transform his ordinary longing and unremarkable maleness into a thing of great beauty: the very embodiment of the Erotic Mother.

What is the mechanism of transvestic alchemy? It is the old elixir of visualization and intense pleasure. Visualization has been variously called self-hypnosis, autosuggestion, enchantment, magic, self-fulfilling prophecy, and imagination. The secret of successful visualization is to link it to intense feelings of pleasure and well-being—something the CD does very well.

When he cross-dresses, the CD is trying to give life to the Erotic Mother through visualization and pleasure. The CD spends so much time in front of the mirror not because he is especially vain, but because the mirror is the tool of visualization. It is in front of the mirror that the CD can see himself being transformed into the mother. The CD's brain assists him in this task, for it filters out any unwanted visual information from the image.

The power of the brain to modify visual images to suit a desired belief is well documented; people see what they want to see. This is why the CD sees a beautiful woman when he is alone in front of the mirror. He does not see a penis, body hair, or a male torso. Instead, he has programmed his brain, through self-hypnosis, to process his own image so that what he sees is the ideal woman.

Thanks to this selective processing, the CD often believes himself to look better than he actually does when he is cross-dressed. This illusion sometimes encourages him to venture out into public while dressed as a woman. What the public sees is a man dressed as a woman; what the CD sees is a beautiful woman.

Like the emperor who wore no clothes, the CD also thinks he looks splendid. But just as the emperor had his detractors, there's always a child in the crowd who will yell, "Mommy! That man's wearing a dress!" It's usually at this juncture that the selective processing apparatus collapses back into the normal state and the CD, unless he is an exhibitionist, beats a hasty retreat home.

Nevertheless, when the CD is alone in front of the mirror the mechanism of selective seeing is all-powerful. I think that in the act of cross-dressing the clothes and the cosmetics cue the CD's brain to secrete endorphins; to shift itself into a more relaxed alpha state; to loosen the inhibitory network; to transit into a different cognitive realm.

It might also be that if the CD does indeed have feminized brain structures—which I believe is the case—such structures are activated by the process of cross-dressing. Since brain structures can alter the perception of reality, the CD's sense of himself is altered, or neurologically shifted, so that he attains a state in which he "feels" like a woman.

The incarnation of the Erotic Mother begins during the interlude leading to orgasm. In Money's term, the CD is following his *lovemap*. Where does the CD's lovemap lead? It leads him up to a dimly lit summit where, in the rarefied air of orgasm, he will merge with the Erotic Mother and find complete bliss.

The male orgasm fuels the incarnation of the Erotic Mother by giving her psychosexual force and reality. The Erotic Mother is no fiction to the CD, for he feels her skin when he puts on women's clothing, and he melds into her during orgasm. The transmutation of the male orgasm into an ecstatic union with the Erotic Mother is the mechanism of the alchemy of cross-dressing. From this perspective, cross-dressing can clearly be understood as tantric in nature.

The alchemy of true cross-dressing is potent, for the CD indeed invokes the presence of the Erotic Mother from the deep sky of the collective unconsciousness. However, as any CD who soars into the empyrean soon learns, a mortal cannot love a goddess without paying a price.

When the CD evokes the Erotic Mother, he brings down upon himself hurtful and unintended ironies for which he never bargained. The first irony is that the Mother is attracted to the Father because of his strength and masculinity. Yet the CD sees himself as a feminine male—a being undesirable to the Erotic Mother.

In becoming the image of the Erotic Mother, then, the CD can never really possess her, or for that matter most any other woman, because women do not generally desire feminine men. The ultimate CD fantasy is to find a woman who will completely accept and indulge his behavior—including having sexual relations with him while he is dressed as a woman. Yet the agony of CDs everywhere is that they cannot find such a woman. What they find instead is that their cross-dressing is a barrier between them and the woman they love, particularly if the woman takes the view that his cross-dressing is perverted or somehow competes with her femininity.

In attempting to incarnate the Erotic Mother, the CD typically encounters rejection from real women. This rejection compounds the CD's image of himself as a weak man, and ironically reinforces his need to cross-dress. He gains pleasure from cross-dressing only to later despise himself and feel ashamed. In the face of this stark dissonance, the CD's temporal, triumphant union with the Erotic Mother is flawed by loneliness. He is suddenly, and only, a lonely man who wears women's clothing.

The second unintended irony is reserved for those CDs who go beyond mere clothing and seek to incarnate the Erotic Mother in her sexual role. To the extent that the CD wants the assurance that he embodies the Erotic Mother, he will seek the same thing that most women look for to assure their femininity: the love and embrace of a man.

When such a CD is having sex with a man, he is imagining himself to be a beautiful woman, to be the Erotic Mother, and a man's penis in him is the verification that he has indeed become her. The Erotic Mother seems to live vicariously through the CD when he submits to a man. While this is not well-known, some CDs report a sense of being "possessed" by the spirit of a woman when they are having sex with a man. They claim that a libidinous female spirit overtakes them and subverts their bodies to her purposes. From a metaphysical point of view, these reports are provocative and have some basis in the sexual lore of spirituality.

However, despair often arises when the enchantment ends, for the CD has not only violated the male caste system by having sex with another man, but he has doubly compounded the offense by dressing as a woman while doing so. The second irony, then, is that when the CD tries to incarnate the Erotic Mother in her sexual role, he alienates himself from the male metaculture in general, and the affections of women in particular, for what woman wishes to be involved with a bisexual transvestite?

Of course this last point does not apply to the gay CD whose motivation is to be a feminine man submitting to a masculine man (or to be a feminine man dominating a masculine man). In such cases, the issues of submission and power are being played out in a context of lust and symbolism.

The final irony of the search for the Erotic Mother is when the CD lies down upon the sacrificial altar to gain the ultimate emblem of identification: a vagina. The transsexual becomes the Erotic Mother when he, in an act of worship, in an act of returning to his source, makes his body like hers. Yet in giving up his penis to become the Erotic Mother, the TS often becomes a woman who craves masculine strength and fertility. The final irony is that the very thing the transsexual renounces in himself is the very thing she looks for in her new life.

Of course, not all post-op transsexuals seek a relationship with a man. Some desire a "lesbian" relationship with a woman. But in this case, even the "Mother Goddess" literature of lesbianism indicates that lesbians are seeking a metaphysical and sexual bond with the

Earth Mother via the bodies and souls of other women. And who is the Mother Goddess except a Sapphic analogue of the Erotic Mother?

FETISHISM REVISITED

In this section, I want to revisit fetishism with a view toward uncovering the true nature of gender. I begin by noting that an opinion I've had for some time holds that if all of the distinctions between masculinity and femininity were erased, cross-dressing, or some form of it, would continue to exist.

Given that the desire to possess the Erotic Mother represents a key aspect of cross-dressing, it follows that CDs would be predisposed to seek the Erotic Mother by using whatever sort of symbols of femininity were available. Of course, such symbolic seeking would be considered fetishistic—which brings us back into the circle of gender. Can we ever get outside of this circle?

The missionary asserts that when the shaman realizes that belief alone is all that makes the fetish powerful, the shaman will no longer be a prisoner to the fetish; he will be free to worship the true Christian God. The psychologist claims that when the twentieth-century neurotic sees that he has falsely assigned his erotic feelings to an article of clothing, he can renounce this practice, reorient his orgasmic fantasies, and have normal sexual relations.

Reasonable as such claims seem, they arrogantly assume that a missionary or psychoanalyst, by virtue of a superior doctrine or mind, is in a position to authoritatively pronounce another's religion or sexuality fetishistic. Yet if the shoe were on the other foot, so to speak, the missionary would become livid if he were asked to renounce the Cross as fetishistic. Likewise, the psychoanalyst would be outraged if she were asked to characterize the Ph.D. on her office wall as a fetish whose power derived only from her belief in it.

The indictment of fetishism argues that it is abnormal for a person to have an erotic or spiritual relationship to certain objects. Yet fetishism is often nothing more than an indictment pressed by those in power who do not like certain forms of expression; it is but an antagonistic negation of another's unconventional use of symbols and/or sensuality.

The clinical injunction against fetishism implicitly argues that we should somehow be rationally unaffected by objects. But this is sterile and unfeeling. Humans have complex relationships to objects, symbols, and clothing. So it should not be surprising that we imbue many objects with great emotional and sexual significance.

Whether it's a jet-black Lamborghini Diablo, a red silk bra hanging on a brass bedpost, lilacs on a jade satin comforter, a fully armed F-14 glistening in the Mediterranean sky, or a sunken marble tub filled with scented water and rose petals, the fact is that certain objects have the power to elicit passion, to excite the eye, and to evoke lust.

It seems, however, that psychology wants to draw a sensory line that must not be crossed. It's as if we are allowed to enjoy our sensory experience of objects until we reach the point where such enjoyment becomes erotic or somehow too fascinating, and then we are commanded to stop lest we be diagnosed as fetishistic.

But our world is too full of silken beds, alluring scents, beautiful art, sensuous clothing, supple textures, delicious food, cold champagne, and thrilling machines to limit our sensual involvement with the objects that surround us.

Our relationship with objects begins in early childhood when we're given a stuffed animal to comfort us. *The stuffed animal begins the process whereby we are intuitively taught to look to objects for the satisfaction of our needs.* Indeed, an important element of childhood education is in learning what objects are, how they work, and what they can offer in terms of gratification.

If you've given your child a Nintendo or a Sega Genesis game, you know the feeling of being constantly badgered to buy $60 game cartridges. Small children quickly learn to desire objects, particularly toys and candy, because such objects stimulate their senses.

From needing the teddy bear to feel safe at night, we grow to believe that if we can acquire certain objects we will be happy. We are taught to look to objects to meet our needs. If you have a headache, you take a pill. If you're unhappy, you go buy something. If you can buy a bigger house or a better car, you can be happier. This process is often ridiculed as soulless consumerism, yet this indictment misses the profundity underlying the need: We seek objects to make us feel secure, happy, and fulfilled.

If you're a parent, then you know the joy of giving your children gifts on Christmas, Hanukkah, or their birthday. The joy of parental giving reinforces a child's budding relationship to objects, for receiving gifts makes the child happy.

Gift giving is an emotional expression of caring that is expressed through a material object. Its message is simple: I love you—here's a splendid object that I think will make you feel good. Is this wrong? Certainly not, for we live in a material world and so one's choices are limited to either giving a material gift or an intangible gift. In most cases, people choose material gifts because that is usually what the recipient wants, expects, or needs.

The lesson of gift-giving is love. Love can be expressed materially. We feel loved when we get things, and we express our love when we give things. Gifts are a medium of emotional exchange. Indeed, the lesson we teach children is that it is the thought, and not the gift, that really counts.

Clothing is also medium of emotional exchange. We wear clothes that make us feel good and that will make us attractive to others. Part of the fun of shopping for clothes is that it makes you feel good to find things that will make you feel sexy or attractive. Clothing can easily arouse passion, especially when one's partner is attractively dressed.

The clinical taboo against sexual fetishism fails to grasp the emotional satisfaction that wearing desirable clothing offers. But psychology in general fails to understand the passion of the world and the objects therein. Like an uptight, clueless schoolmaster with horn-rimmed glasses, psychology seems to think that people should have emotionless, detached relationships to all objects, including clothing.

But people don't. People drive a particular car because they want to make a statement. They own fur coats because fur coats feel luxurious—and they don't care if animals have to die for this luxury. People own guns because guns make them feel safe and offer them a sense of lethal power they wouldn't otherwise possess. People love their possessions, struggle to acquire beautiful and comfortable things, and even die to protect their objects.

We are attached to our objects, or more properly, our material goods. However, when a person's relationship to an object, or objects, exceeds what is considered normal, certain implications arise. For example, one is considered to be *materialistic* when he devotes an undue amount of time and attention to acquiring material goods.

But materialism is relative; it is often no more than an accusation lobbed at someone who has something another doesn't. Likewise, what the fetishist is doing is really no different from what anyone else is doing: He is having a complex, emotional relationship to an object. The person who has the capacity to sexually enjoy clothing is hardly different from others, for we all are capable of deriving complex forms of gratification from our involvement with any number of physical objects.

SYMBOLS AND ARTIFACTS

In order to understand the nature of fetishism we need to contrast it with both symbols and artifacts. Because we live in a physical world, we must relate to physical objects. Most of these objects are utilitarian, such as can openers, phones, computers, or automobiles. Others, such as pleasure boats or slot machines, are used for play. Heart-lung machines or guided missiles are types of objects used only by specialists for extreme purposes.

There is an entire class of physical objects, however, that go beyond being merely objects. These are symbols. Symbols represent such things as institutions, meanings, or spiritual beliefs. In our modern age, the most common symbols are visual images. These may be printed, displayed electronically, or rendered as signs. Many visual images, called logos, are used to symbolize corporations and products. Other visual images, such as flags, are used to symbolize institutions, governments, and countries. The American flag and Mickey Mouse are outstanding examples of well-known symbols.

Because we are physical and God is considered to be spiritual, or nonphysical, the only way we can physically represent God is through religious symbols, such as the cross or the Star of David. Religious symbols are said to point to God, much in the same way that a road sign points to a given destination.

Medicine is symbolized by the image of two serpents coiled around a stake. The movie industry uses the Oscar statuette to symbolize and acknowledge the best efforts in cinema. Law enforcement uses badges to symbolize its power to maintain order and arrest lawbreakers. The throne of England is symbolized by a crown and scepter. Whether they connote the Teamsters, the Nobel Prize, the Rotary Club, the state of Montana, or Ford Motor Company, symbols are an essential element of human communication: they convey meaning nonverbally.

Humans originate and use symbols to communicate many types of meaning. Our relationship to symbols is emotional and often not entirely rational, for we equate symbols with the very thing for which they stand. When the American flag is burned or disgraced, for instance, many Americans feel that they are being personally insulted and that the offense should be avenged with violence.

Consider the outrage that erupted when an artist immersed an inverted cross in a jar of urine. The desecration of the symbol of Christ's suffering was condemned as evil by believers everywhere. To invert the cross is an ancient satanic practice used to mock Christ. To further mock Christ by immersing an inverted cross in urine makes a powerful, blasphemous statement to those who understand and worship the meaning behind the cross.

There exists a strong sense of propriety with respect to most symbols, for symbols mean something and people feel that those meanings should be respected. There is a distinct difference, however, between symbols and artifacts.

Although artifacts don't carry the weighty meaning of symbols, they are obviously more vital to our survival. Thus, one can burn the flag with virtual impunity but he had better not damage the government building in front of which he does it unless he wants the FBI coming after him!

This odd contradiction reveals the often paper-thin veneer of symbols. It is reasonable to concede that the flag is only a piece of cloth and that burning it cannot destroy the meaning it represents. Burning the flag is simply a statement to show hostility for American policies. America is not made less when her flag is burned—unless you are one for whom symbols are more important than freedom of expression.

President Bush wanted to make it a crime to burn the flag. That desecrating a symbol could be considered a crime takes us to the dubious boundary where freedom of expression becomes taboo when our sense of symbolism is offended. This is the exact boundary the crossdresser transgresses when he puts on an article of women's clothing or achieves sexual gratification from it. I contend that, in both the popular and clinical sense, the notion of sexual fetishism, as well as our uneasiness with cross-dressing, reflects a sense of trespass against the symbols of femininity.

CLOTHING: ARTIFACT, SYMBOL, OR FETISH?

As we discussed earlier, feminism considers women's clothing to be artifactual. Yet psychology argues that women's clothing has symbolic value, and that the violation of that symbolism is what constitutes fetishism and cross-dressing. After all, if there weren't "women's clothing" then could there be fetishism or cross-dressing?

This distinction presents a conundrum. On the one hand, women's clothing and cosmetics must be seen as artifactual in order to free women from being defined merely by such artifacts. On the other hand, those psychologists who wish to attribute the weight of symbology to women's clothing and cosmetics to explain the behavior of the fetishist and CD ironically perpetuate the definition of woman-as-a-collection-of-artifacts.

In giving fetishism symbolic meaning, psychology is essentially saying that clothing and cosmetics embody the meaning of women. Yet it is demeaning to argue that one half of the human population can be symbolized by mere apparel—but this is an important way in which the sexes are divided.

Gender, like God, does not exist physically. It cannot be located or quantified. Rather, it exists as a series of cultural conventions about how men and women should think, act, and dress. Because it is nonphysical, gender can only be represented by symbols, the most obvious one being clothing.

The present concepts of sexual fetishism and cross-dressing are problematic because they're rooted in an ambivalent view of women's clothing. But culture and psychology can't have it both ways: Either women's clothing is merely artifactual or it symbolizes the very essence of women.

Cross-dressing and fetishism exist only because we use clothing to symbolize women. Yet such symbolism is the exact thing that feminism seeks to negate because it dehumanizes women. Understood from this point of view, fetishism and cross-dressing can finally be seen as nothing more than the reductio ad absurdum of defining women by their clothing.

THE SORCERY OF GENDER

The devil in all of this is our cultural inability to recognize true fetishism when it's staring us in the face. If there is a true fetish in our culture, it is gender. Gender is a psychological fetish that society has imbued with great symbolic power. The word *fetish* is derived from the Latin *facere*, which is the root word for the Latin words *facticius* and *factitius*, which denote that which is fictitious. *Facere* also is the root of the word *artifact*, the term we've been using to characterize those objects that denote masculinity or femininity.

The intriguing links between the words *fetish*, *artifact*, and *fiction* can be used to suggest that gender, to the extent that it is based upon artifacts, is a fiction. And if the artifacts of gender are fictional, then the concept of sexual fetishism is also a fiction. *Facere* also serves as the root of the Portuguese *feitiço*, which denotes a charm or the act of sorcery. Hence, we can draw the implication that to assign the quality of gender to artifacts such as clothing is a form of cultural sorcery.

The word *symbol* derives from the Greek *symbolon* and denotes a token, a pledge, or a sign by which one infers a thing. The artifacts of gender are the tokens we use to infer masculinity and femininity. The problem, however, is that these tokens have become fetishes, and, as

Dr. Freud said in *Three Essays on the Theory of Sexuality,* "the situation becomes pathological when the longing for the *fetish* takes the place of the *normal aim* and becomes the *sole object of desire.*"

While the normal aim of culture should be freedom of individual expression, our gender fetish has instead become culture's sole object of desire: We want men to be masculine and women to be feminine. The question facing culture is this: Do we wish to break the spell?

THE RECONFIGURATION OF CULTURE

To break the spell of gender requires expanding the horizons of masculinity and femininity beyond the boundaries of anatomy. Is culture prepared to do such a thing? The growth of humanity has always depended upon bold ideas that offer increased personal freedom, self-determination, and self-expression. Renaissance, reformation, and revolution occurred as natural outgrowths of protest. And so it is that another reconfiguration of culture is upon us.

Reconfiguration is my term for the broad, unstructured series of events and ideas that have altered society over the last thirty years. The central factor of this movement has been the steadfast refusal by many individuals to fit into the traditional mold dictated by church and state. From New Age teachings to the rise of new business thinking, the message has been that people must have much more freedom of thought, expression, time, occupation, and relationship than they have previously throughout the centuries. And just as the printing press favored the masses in the past, so, too, is technology still in our favor.

From the Internet, to desktop publishing, to genetic engineering, technology is poised to launch humanity into an uncharted dimension of existence. A reconfiguration of our basic ideas about ourselves is needed if we are to become large enough to encompass the possibilities offered by technology.

Reconfiguration is quite different from negation. In reconfiguration one doesn't destroy the old ideas, but they are reassessed, reprioritized, and reordered. Just as genetic engineering is forcing us to reconfigure our ideas about medicine, ethics, agriculture, and manufacturing, so, too, are people such as enterpreneurs, artists, and the transgendered forcing us to reconfigure our ideas about the economy, culture, and gender. Indeed, we have never been closer in history to completely reordering our ideas about such things as family, work, gender, biology, technology, and homosexuality than we are right now.

As we prepare to enter the new millennium, the CD is in league with a host of other agents of change. All of this is part of a grand and irresistible force of evolution acting to push out the borders of human consciousness. Where will it all end, this push for change and growth?

Who knows? For the human mind is vast, the need of people to express themselves great, and the pace of scientific and psychological discovery ever on the increase. The only way to keep up with the change and growth of the world is to change and grow with it—and that demands tolerance for a wide range of behaviors, ideas, and challenges that a person may not necessarily endorse.

The only possible way to accommodate such changes in a practical sense is to reaffirm the ideals of democracy. The individual must fundamentally recognize that the best way to keep his freedom is to allow others to have theirs. The Madisonian notion that society needs a multiplicity of interests to counterbalance each other is particularly useful at this time in history.

The cultural war between secular humanism and religious fundamentalism, for instance, need not be seen as a battle to the death. Rather, it can be viewed as one expected outcome of a free society. If anything, we are fortunate to have the freedom whereby the two factions may counterbalance each other. If either side did gain the upper hand, we would suffer the abysmal tyranny of dogmatists.

An aspect of the debate between secularism and fundamentalism is highlighted by the issue of gay rights. My friend Cindy wants the freedom to legally marry her partner, Kay. Conversely, fundamentalists would like to give prayer and creation science a place in public schools. Are such demands mutually exclusive?

No. In fact, they've never been. Only our absolutist beliefs have made them contradictory. As long as people choose to negotiate rather than destroy each other, it is always possible to balance "mutually exclusive" positions. The essence of the democratic process is to achieve a peaceful coexistence among a multiplicity of interests. By recognizing the fundamental rights of one another, we avoid bloodshed, though we certainly don't always attain the "ideal" society.

The idea of the CD, and other radical elements, as evolutionary agents of consciousness who force a constant reconfiguration of cultural norms speaks to the emerging panculture of tolerance that is becoming increasingly required—particularly in the global economy. Just as the global economy must tolerate the diversity of individual cultures if it is to exist, so, too, must the diversity of the individual be tolerated if humanity is to flourish.

Cross-dressing is but a small tile in the vast mosaic of human behavior. Still, under the heading of "the pursuit of happiness" the transgendered deserve the same freedom of expression as do those who enjoy other versions of happiness. In any case, the future happiness of each of us demands that we work to ensure a society in which freedom is not held captive to fanaticism nor the fear of that which is different.

I trust that I will live to see the day when male cross-dressing is viewed as unremarkable. I look forward to the day when I'll be able to go to a party and have someone say, "That's a beautiful dress, you look very nice," and leave it at that. After all, a good dress is expensive—and is a guy so wrong for wanting a compliment on his appearance?

Support Groups for Cross-Dressers and Transgenderists

Note: This list is current as of the date of writing. The author assumes no liability for its accuracy.

National Organizations

International Federation for Gender Education (IFGE)
P.O. Box 229
Waltham, MA 02154-0229
Phone: (617) 894-8340
Fax: (617) 899-5703
E-mail: IFGE@world.std.com

The Society for the Second Self (Tri-Ess)

Tri-Ess has chapters in many states. For the one nearest you, write or call:
Tri-Ess	Tri-Ess
P.O. Box 194	8880 Bellaire B2, Suite 104
Tulare, CA 93275	Houston, TX 77036
(209) 688-9246	(713) 988-8064

American Educational Gender Information Service (AEGIS)
P.O. Box 33724
Decatur, GA 30033-0724
(404) 939-0244

Renaissance Education Association, Inc.
P.O. Box 60552
King of Prussia, PA 19406
(214) 630-1347

212 • SUPPORT GROUPS

Regional Organizations

Androgyny
P.O. Box 480740
Los Angeles, CA 90048
(213) 467-8317

Atlanta Gender Exploration (AGE)
P.O. Box 77562
Atlanta, GA 30357
(404) 875-9846

Boulton and Park Society
P.O. Box 17
Bulverde, TX 78163
(210) 980-7788

Crossroads
P.O. Box 1245
Royal Oak, MI 48068-1245
(313) 537-3267

Crossdressers and Friends (CAF)
Box 4092
Overland Park, KS 66204
(913) 791-3947

Crossdressers International (CDI)
P.O. Box 50192
Tulsa, OK 74104
(918) 582-6643
(918) 835-5334

Cross-Dressers of New York/NYGA
c/o Muriel Olive
9 W. 31st Street, Suite 7R
New York, NY 10001
(212) 570-7389

Cross-Port
Box 54657
Cincinnati, OH 45254-0657
(513) 474-9557

ETVC (Educational TV Channel)
P.O. Box 426486
San Francisco, CA 94142-6486
(510) 549-2665

Fantasia
c/o GLCS
Box 533446
Orlando, FL 32853-3446
(407) 425-4527

Gender Identity Center of
Colorado (GIC)
3715 W. 32nd Avenue
Denver, CO 80211
(303) 458-5378

Phoenix Transgender Support
P.O. Box 18332
Asheville, NC 28814
(704) 259-9428

Powder Puffs of California (PPOC)
P.O. Box 1088
Yorba Linda, CA
(714) 779-9013

Renaissance, South Jersey Chapter
P.O. Box 189
Mays Landing, NJ 08330
(609) 435-5401

Renaissance, Greater Philadelphia
Chapter
P.O. Box 530
Bensalem, PA 19020
(610) 630-1437

Society of Cross-Dressing
Hardware Engineers
276 Pearl St. #L
Cambridge, MA 02139

Tennessee Vals
P.O. Box 92355
Nashville, TN
(615) 664-6883

Tiffany Club of New England
P.O. Box 2283
Waltham, MA 01888-0483
(617) 891-9325

Transpitt
P.O. Box 3214
Pittsburgh, PA 15230
(412) 231-1181

Washington/Baltimore Alliance
c/o R. Lewis
P.O. Box 50724
Washington D.C. 20091-0724
(301) 277-5475

An Internet address for information about issues of interest to the transgendered community is http://www.tgforum.com /

The author can be e-mailed on the Internet at: jjallen@ix.netcom.com

PUBLICATIONS FOR THE CROSS-DRESSER

Cross-Talk is a monthly magazine published by Kimberleigh Richards. *Cross-Talk* is a useful compendium of current information, opinion, and humor gleaned from the newsletters of CD support groups across the United States. For subscription information write to: *Cross-Talk*; P.O. Box 944; Woodland Hills, CA 91365.

Dragazine must be seen to be believed. It's too fun a magazine not to leave out on your coffee table. Write to: *Dragazine*; P.O. Box 619664; West Hollywood, CA 90069.

Ladylike is a quarterly magazine dealing with the CD scene. It is a quality publication featuring photos, reader-written stories and letters, and personal ads. Write to: Creative Design Services; P.O. Box 1263; King of Prussia, PA 19406.

Nugget is a fetish-oriented monthly magazine worth mentioning because of its transsexual columnist, Haley Tiresius. In her column "Tiresius Knows," Haley serves as a sort of Dear Abby to the transgendered. She dispenses common-sense advice about often unusual sexual problems. *Nugget* is available wherever adult publications are sold, or write to: *Nugget*; 2600 Douglas Road, Suite 600; Coral Gables, FL 33134.

Reflections is the glossy magazine of Mistress Antoinette, a well-known dominatrix. The publication is devoted to America's three favorite subjects: fetish fashions, bondage and discipline, and cross-dressing. For information write c/o Versatile Fashions; P.O. Box 1051; Tustin, CA 92681

Transgender magazine is the flagship of transgendered publications. It is an articulate magazine written by laypeople and professionals. One must read it to stay at the cutting edge of transgenderism. For information write to IFGE; P.O. Box 367; Wayland, MA 01778.

Sandy Thomas Publications has a large catalogue of CD fantasy literature. For information write: Sandy Thomas Publications; P.O. Box 2309; Capistrano Beach, CA 92624-0309.

TV Epic is a sexually oriented monthly magazine devoted to personal advertisements and photographs. Available at adult bookstores or from Pathway Communications; 105 Serra Way; Milpitas, CA 95035.

BIBLIOGRAPHY

Begley, Sharon. "Gray Matters." *Newsweek,* March 27, 1995, p. 48.

Bettelheim, Bruno. *Symbolic Wounds.* Chicago: Free Press, 1954.

Bornstein, Kate. *Gender Outlaw: On Men, Women and the Rest of Us.* New York: Vintage Books, 1994.

Bullough, Vern L., and Bonnie Bullough. *Cross-Dressing, Sex and Gender.* Philadelphia: University of Pennsylvania Press, 1993.

Docter, Richard F. *Transvestites and Transsexuals: Toward a Theory of Cross-Gender Behavior,* New York: Plenum Press, 1993.

D'Souza, Dinesh. *The End of Racism.* New York: Free Press, 1995.

Freud, Sigmund. *Three Essays on the Theory of Sexuality.* New York: Basic Books, 1962.

Garber, Marjorie. *Vested Interests: Cross-Dressing and Cultural Anxiety.* New York: Routledge, Chapman and Hall, 1992.

Hirschfeld, Magnus. *Die Transvestiten: Eine Untersuchung über den erotishen Verkleidungsteib.* Berlin: Alfred Pulvermacher, 1910. Tr. Michael Lombardi-Nash. *Transvestites: The Erotic Drive to Cross Dress.* New York: Prometheus Books, 1991.

———. *Sexual Anomalies: The Origins, Nature, and Treatment of Sexual Disorders.* New York: Emerson Books, 1956.

International Bill of Gender Rights. Adopted by the Second International Conference of Transgender Law and Employment Policy. Houston, Tex., August 23, 1993.

Kaplan, Louise. *Female Perversions: The Temptations of Emma Bovary.* New York: Doubleday Books, 1991.

Laplanche, Jean, and J. B. Pontalis. *The Language of Psycho-Analysis,* tr. Donald Micholson-Smith. New York: W. W. Norton, 1974.

Lynn, Merissa Sherrill. Quoted in International Federation for Gender Education, publicity brochure and membership application, Waltham, Mass., 1995.

Millet, Kate. *Sexual Politics.* New York: Doubleday Books, 1969.

Money, John, and Patricia Allen. *Sexual Signatures: On Being a Man or a Woman.* Boston: Little, Brown, 1975.

———. *Gay, Straight and In-Between: The Sexology of Erotic Orientation.* New York: Oxford University Press, 1988.

Prince, Virginia. Quoted in *Transvestia Magazine*, no. 12, 1963. "The Intent and Purpose of *Transvestia*," (reprinted by permission of Sandy Thomas Publications; Capistrano Beach, Cal., 1995).

———. Quoted in *Transvestia Magazine*, no. 100, 1976 (reprinted by permission of Sandy Thomas Publications; Capistrano Beach, Cal., 1995).

Raymond, Janice G. *The Transsexual Empire: The Making of the She-Male.* Boston: Beacon Press, 1979.

Rothblatt, Martine. *The Apartheid of Sex: A Manifesto on the Freedom of Gender.* New York: Crown Publishers, 1995.